The Key To

DREAM ANALYSIS

A Dreamstairway Book

The Key To

DREAM ANALYSIS

By

Ray Douglas

British Library Cataloguing in Publication Data.
A catalogue record for this book is available from the British Library.

First published on-line in the UK by Dreamstairway 2006
This paperback edition published by Dreamstairway in 2009

© Ray Douglas 2006 and 2009

ISBN 978-1-907091-01-8

CONTENTS

General Information

A useful source of everything you will need to know concerning your dream life. You will be led to many of the categories through a system of cross-references.

Dream Symbols

Anything identifiable in your dream will most likely be a symbol. Look up the meaning of this symbol and think all round it very carefully. You will be led by cross-references to any further categories which may prove helpful in your final interpretation.

Theme Moods

If you experienced any strong emotion during your dream, or afterwards when you awoke, this will be very important. Try to relive the dream and recall all your feelings about it. The theme mood sometimes changes during the course of the dream, perhaps from worry to relief, or from puzzlement to reassurance, and this will be very significant.

Everything in the book is arranged in alphabetical order for quick and easy reference. For a more detailed list of categories please refer to the Index.

Index   page 229

About the author   page 234

General Information Paragraphs

Acting out the dream
Active and passive roles
Adlerian dreams
Analysing dreams
Animal-nature dreams
Archetypes
Association of ideas
Balancing dreams
Biblical dreams
Children's dreams
Collective intelligence
Collective unconscious mind
Compensatory dreams
Conscientious dreams
Controlling dreams
Cycle of creation in dreams
Cycle of the dreaming self
Dawn dreams
Development of dreams
Diagrams of the dreaming self
Disaster dreams
Disgusting dreams
Disorientated dreams
Dozing dreams
Drawing a dream
Dream diagrams
Ego overruled in a dream
Enacting dreams in company
Encouraging dreams
Endo-psychic censor
Evening dreams
Everyday dreams
Family-intuitive dreams
Free association
Freudian dreams
Frightening dreams
Future coming to awareness
Great dreams
Group dream-therapy
Healing dreams
Holistic understanding
Impersonal dreams
Incubating dreams
Inner feelings
Interpreting dreams for others
Inter-reactive dreams
Intuitive dreams

Jekyll and Hyde dreams
Jungian dreams
Lucid dreams
Mandala diagrams
Meditation
Morality
Mythmaking dreams
Nightmares
Non-self dreams
Paralysis in sleep
Persona
Personal dreams
Personal unconscious mind
Plant-nature dreams
Predictive dreams
Purifying dreams
Questionnaire
Rapid eye movement
Recording dreams
Recurrent dreams
Re-entering a dream
Regression
Reincarnation dreams
Relationship dreams
Repression dreams
Selection of images
Self
Sexual dreams
Shadow
Sharing of dreams
Spherical symbols of the self
Submission of will
Symbolic nature of dreams
Symbols and their origin
Theme mood
Trigger events
Trivial dreams
Veridical dreams
Volitional dreams
Waking dreams
Waking inspirations
Warning dreams
White lie dreams
Wish-fulfilment dreams
World dream
Worried dreams
Yin Yang

Dream Symbols

ABANDONMENT
ABBEY
ABYSS
ABUSE
ACCIDENT
ACCUSATIONS
ACNE
ACROBATICS
ACTING
ADVERSARY
ADVICE
AGILITY
ALTAR
ANGEL
ANGER
ANIMALS
ANTIQUES
ARCHAEOLOGY
ART
ASSAILANT
AUTUMN
BABY
BALL
BALLET
BALLOON
BAMBOO
BARN
BATTLE
BATTLEMENTS
BIRDS
BLOOD
BOAT
BOG
BONES
BOOKS
BREAD
BRIDGE
BROOM
BUGS
BULL

BULLY
BULRUSHES
BURGLAR
BURIAL
CACTUS
CALENDAR
CANDLE
CAR
CARNIVAL
CARVINGS
CATHEDRAL
CAVE
CELLAR
CHASING
CHILD
CHURCH
CLIMBING
CLOCK
CLOTHES
CLOUDS
COCKEREL
CORPSE
COW
CROCODILE
CROSSROADS
CRYSTALS
CUP
DAM
DANCE
DARKNESS
DARTS
DEATH
DEMON
DESERT
DICE
DIGGING
DIRT
DIVING
DOCTOR
DOG

DOLL	HOTEL
DOLPHINS	HURRICANE
DOOR	HUT
DRAGON	IDOL
DRIVING	INCENSE
DROWNING	INSECTS
DUNGEON	JETTY
DUST	JEWELS
EAGLE	JOURNEY
EARTH MOTHER	JUDGE
EARTHQUAKE	JUNCTION
EATING	KING
ECHO	KITE
ECLIPSE	LABYRINTH
EGGS	LADDER
ELEPHANT	LAKE
EMBROIDERY	LAMENESS
EMBRYO	LAUNDRY
ENEMY	LIBRARY
ESCAPING	LILIES
EXAM	LOST
EXCREMENT	LUGGAGE
FACADE	MACHINERY
FACTORY	MANDALA
FALLING	MARKET PLACE
FARM	MIST
FASHIONS	MONSTER
FEAST	MONUMENT
FEET	MOON
FENCE	MOUNTAIN
FISH	MUD
FLOWER	MUSEUM
FLYING	NAKED
FOG	OBSTACLES
FOOD	OPPONENT
GRAVE	PAINTING
HAT	PARALYSIS
HEDGE	PARROT
HERO	PATH
HOLLY	PEARL
HONEY	PIG
HORSE	PIT
HOSPITAL	PLAYING

PLOUGHING	SUNDIAL
POLICE	TEETH
PRECIPICE	THEATRE
PROCESSION	THORNS
QUARREL	THRONE
QUEEN	TIDAL WAVE
RAIL JOURNEY	TOILET
RAINBOW	TOWER
RATS	TREASURE
RIVER	TUNNEL
ROAD	UNEMPLOYMENT
ROCKS	UNIFORM
RUINS	VALLEY
SAND	VASE
SCRAPHEAP	VOLCANO
SEA	WALL
SKELETON	WATER
SNAKE	WEEDING
SNOW AND ICE	WISE PERSON
STATUE	WITCH
STEPPING STONES	WOLF
STONE CIRCLE	XENOPHOBIA
STORE	YOKE
SUN	ZOO

Theme Moods

Acceptance	Hate
Affection	Helplessness
Aggression	Horror
Amusement	Joy
Anger	Laughter
Apprehension	Love
Arrogance	Painful duty
Concern	Pity
Contempt	Puzzlement
Despair	Sadness
Distrust	Tearfulness
Doubt	Terror
Exasperation	Worry
Fearfulness	

THE KEY TO DREAM ANALYSIS

How to use this book

Most people's dreams are centred on everyday affairs, relationships, work and leisure pursuits. But when you start taking an interest in your own dream life, recalling, recording and trying to understand your dreams, their character will change. The dreaming cycle within your personal unconscious mind will kick into action, and your dreams will become deeper and more significant.

Dreams have different layers of meaning. This book will help you to analyse your dreams, but only you can interpret them fully, because only you know about all the memories, incidents and experiences of your own daily life. Start by remembering your dreams and keeping a careful record of them, writing down every detail in sequence, and thinking round them thoroughly.

Look up the sections on *Analysing dreams,* and *Recording dreams.* Then refer to any specific symbols that cropped up in the dream, whether they seemed important or not. Then try to recall your feelings, your mood as you experienced the dream, or immediately after waking, and refer to the appropriate *Theme mood.* The emotions which you felt at the time will give you an important clue about the meaning of the dream.

Let your dream be your teacher, but be honest with yourself. Avoid the temptation to alter or gloss over any details even though you may find them unflattering. Your dreams may refer to your conscious everyday experiences, but they also provide access to the contents of your unconscious mind. If you heed the deepest messages of your dreams, they will certainly have sound advice to offer – advice which will help you along the path of life to achieve higher self awareness and psychic fulfilment.

A

ABANDONMENT   *Shedding of responsibilities*

If it is you being abandoned

This dream may of course relate clearly to some real-life incident, and if it seems to contain no answer or solution it will simply be expressing your own feelings at being let down. If there is no real-life equivalent that you can see, try to recapture the mood of your dream: who or what has abandoned you, and what was your dream situation as a result? The symbol is closely allied to the dream symbol of being lost, and may be pointing out that you have lost your way in life. Again, if there is no obvious meaning involving your career or your family or relationships, the dream is likely to be referring to a spiritual abandonment: in effect, you have abandoned yourself – your own non-material higher self can guide you through life. A dream of this nature drops a hint that you need to seek and follow a more spiritual path, and your dreams will point the way if you study and record them carefully.

If you are abandoning something or someone else

If the dream characters are real people known to you, the meaning of the dream will probably be fairly obvious. The nature of the abandonment may be practical, or emotional. The feeling may have been projected by a person who is feeling abandoned, and you are picking this up in your dream. Perhaps someone who is feeling betrayed needs your help or your friendship; don't let them down! It sometimes happens that the dream is reflecting your own feelings of guilt about something that happened in the past, and over which you had no real control. If there is some way you can make amends, it might be as well to do so. If not, and the feeling of guilt persists, try to feel deeply within yourself that you are not to blame for whatever occurred, and ask yourself for a further dream that will balance your feelings and relieve the sense of guilt.

See also: Encouraging dreams; Incubating dreams;
   LABYRINTH; LOST; *Submission of will*

THE KEY TO DREAM ANALYSIS

ABBEY *An ancient church, large and impressive*

If it is a functioning abbey where services are held

Your own emotions are being reflected by this magnificent building, the timeless seat of grand state occasions, reinforcing a feeling of need for authority and stability. We all need something or somebody to rely on. This dream symbol is expressive of the need for a firm foundation on which to stand, but not in a way that makes any demand on yourself personally.

If the abbey is a picturesque ruin

The dream symbol points out that ancient certainties have been destroyed or allowed to decay to make way for modern ideas – and it probably relates to some recent event that has affected you deeply. Your own mood during the dream will do much to explain its nature: a pious or submissive feeling suggests that you are looking for something that once had reality, something very valuable and beautiful. This 'something' is your own early childhood, for a new-born baby is still attached to the higher world of spirit. The symbol of a ruined abbey may also represent a person – perhaps a parent-figure on whom you used to rely. You may be feeling nostalgic for all the comfort and reassurances you once received but which are no longer available except as fond memories.

If it is a ruined abbey, bleak and ghost-haunted

Great abbeys used to be the centres of power in the land, where tithe barns and the abbot's tax gatherers may have spread fear or resentment among the local population. If your feelings during the dream were unpleasant, search your memory for any real-life *Trigger events* you may have experienced recently. These may have reminded you of an unpleasant type of authority that you were glad to get rid of. Some people have unpleasant memories of their schooldays, and this type of dream could recall those times, particularly if something or someone seems to be trying to establish a similarly unpleasant authority over you.

THE KEY TO DREAM ANALYSIS

If it is a romantic ivy-clad Gothic ruin

In warm sunlight, or perhaps by moonlight, a building of this type is a perfect place for romance. Your feelings during the dream will give you a clue, especially if you had companions in the dream: are these people known to you or unknown? Are they real people, or purely imaginary? This could be no more than a *Wish fulfilment dream* in which the beautiful abbey is seen as a beauty spot suitable for a romantic liaison.

See also: ALTAR; CATHEDRAL; CHURCH; RUINS

ABUSE   *Casting blame and insults*

If someone is hurling abuse at you

There may be a hidden element of self-criticism involved in this dream. Have you deserved censure in some way? It may be that the person in the dream is complaining about something which you know does not deserve blame: in this case your dream is being kind to your feelings by disguising the real complaint. You may have been feeling guilty, at a deep level, and blaming yourself about something that is not featured in your dream – something for which you were indeed to blame. Try using *Free association* to find out what it really is: this could be your own subconscious way of concealing your true guilt, by acting out a dream charade.

If you are hurling abuse at someone else

This probably does not relate to any actual incident, but if the person is known to you in real life, you may have hurt their feelings in some way, perhaps inadvertently, and these are the feelings you are picking up in the dream. Dreams are seldom interested in blaming other people or complaining about them treating you unfairly; their chief purpose is to observe and correct your own actions and reactions. Hurting people's feelings can do more harm than one might suppose; the hurt penetrates to a very deep level and reflects back on you!

See also: ACCUSATIONS, ANGER

THE KEY TO DREAM ANALYSIS

ABYSS *A great gaping hole in the ground*

If you have just discovered an abyss

The dream is bringing you to the awareness of your own unconscious mind. You may find yourself remembering things that happened to you many years ago and which you had completely forgotten; or, equally, you may be in danger of ignoring or neglecting responsibilities that other people have thrust upon you. Remember the unpleasant as well as the pleasant things that happen, and learn from them rather than trying to shut them out.

If you are looking down into a dream abyss

Take note of your feelings, your mood, during this dream episode. Whatever your feelings about the abyss, they reflect your habitual attitude towards your own most deeply hidden characteristics. *Trigger events* may have occurred recently which reminded you subconsciously of old patterns of behaviour, long forgotten. Their influence is still active deep inside you!

If you are almost falling into the abyss

This dream may be warning you to tread more carefully in some real life situation. Perhaps your present course of action or pattern of behaviour is threatening to end in disaster. A hole into which you seem in danger of falling can symbolise problems with relationships: you may be in danger of losing your job, or of going 'over the edge' in some very real way. Take careful stock of your current situation in life. If there seem to be no real life people in the dream, it could be that you have become over-attached to logical solutions, or become too dependent upon rules and moral principles. Some situations in life need a sentimental approach, with sympathetic understanding.

If you are actually falling into the dream abyss

The dream is telling you that you are being swamped by the contents of your own unconscious mind. You may have been feeling guilty over things that happened – perhaps long ago, perhaps recently – but it

THE KEY TO DREAM ANALYSIS

is up to you now to put matters right. Take careful note of any people known to you who might have appeared in the dream, because they are sure to be closely involved in these matters. Incidents can seem trivial to the waking mind but will be important to the inner self.

If you are throwing rubbish into the abyss

This dream means that you have been neglecting to deal with matters that need your personal attention. You have probably been pushing unpleasant thoughts or onerous duties away, or perhaps you have been putting blame on someone else when it would make you much happier and better balanced if you faced up to these matters and dealt with them yourself.

If something or someone is pushing you into the abyss

It is important to identify the people or things or animals featuring in the dream, because in waking life they are probably being wrongly treated by you: they are asking you to search your conscience; you may have been ignoring their needs when you could well be dealing with them and their problems more positively.

If you are pushing a person or an animal into the abyss

The implication is that you are ignoring or hurting these people or animals in real life. It may even be an *Archetype of the unconscious mind* which you do not wish to face. You are trying to push these things out of your mind, but they and the problems they represent will not just disappear; they need to be dealt with by you firmly but kindly in real life. If not, unpleasant memories and guilt-feelings will return to haunt you when you are least expecting it.

If you are actually inside the abyss and searching around

Especially if there are other creatures down there, the dream implies that you are 'soul-searching'– exploring your own deeply hidden contents – which is probably showing itself in real life as depression. Your conscious mind may suffer a set-back, but in the long run the experience should be of great value to you. I believe that the dreaming process is working to help make us what might be called whole, fully integrated people, and a dream abyss is really a part of your own psyche that should be familiar to you.

If there are monsters or demons stirring in the abyss

We all have faults, peculiarities and feelings of guilt, though these may have been hidden since childhood. Some *Trigger event* will have happened to bring these forgotten characteristics back to your awareness. Dream monsters like this are usually connected with sex impulses. Thinking quietly about them may make their true identity clear, and then you will be able to do something positive to clear out those old demons.

See also: CAVE; CELLAR; *Collective unconscious;* DUNGEON; *Personal unconscious;* PIT

Acceptance (A theme mood)

If you experienced a powerful emotion during the dream, or a significant part of the dream, this can be call the theme mood. If this mood seemed to be one of resignation or acceptance, it shows that you can trust the dream and put your faith in its message. It is pointing to a positive message which has already been accepted by your *inner feelings,* but probably not yet by your everyday, outer feelings. Try to analyse the dream in the usual way, bearing this mood in mind. Have reliance on whatever conclusion you reach, for it probably has something very valuable to convey. Try to look on the dream-source as something higher than your own conscious awareness, and accept it as an unknown place from which wisdom is to be gleaned.

ACCIDENT   *An unexpected disruption to your progress*

If you dream of an accident while going about your everyday business

If in the dream you are on the move, by foot or bicycle or public transport, this has the nature of a *Warning dream*. An accident or near-accident implies that you are in danger of suffering some sort of material loss, or of running up against financial or legal problems. Analyse the dream and if necessary use your *Association of ideas* to help you think round the possibilities. Take careful note of your feelings and note the theme mood during the dream or immediately after waking; powerful emotions may contain a hint about the severity of the dream accident should it prove to have a counterpart in waking life. To be forewarned is to be forearmed.

If you have an accident while driving

Most dreams of accidents involve driving, especially if a car is your usual mode of transport – and even more so if it is your usual way of getting to work each morning. Cars, mechanical travel in general, or even simple metal objects, are all symbols of materiality, and in dreams they usually represent your own normal progress through life. When you dream there is an accident, or a near miss, or if there seems to be a strong risk of a possible accident, the implication is that either you or those who depend upon you are at risk of facing material loss. This is certainly a *Warning dream,* though its implications may be purely abstract. If you have been pursuing a risky course in real life, use the dream to good advantage by taking heed of the warning. A railway crossing or road junction is often the scene of a dream accident, and this implies that someone else, possibly someone in competition with you, will be closely involved. A car crash or near miss involving a train at a crossing implies that your 'private' vehicle has run up against opposition from a 'public' vehicle. In this case you may assume that legal difficulties are a distinct possibility.

If you dream that someone else has damaged your car

This kind of accident, caused by others but involving your own means of travel through life, implies that people who rely on you in some way are entangling you in their private problems. You may have let your property or goods out to some other person, and the implications then will be fairly obvious. Or if someone related to you, a son or daughter perhaps, is involved in some enterprise that you have struggled to build up, there is a grave danger that they will cause harm to your affairs through their negligence.

See also: CAR; DRIVING; ROAD

THE KEY TO DREAM ANALYSIS

ACCUSATIONS *Ascribing blame*

If you dream that you are accusing someone

Some deep-seated personal fears or worries on your part are being aired in this dream, and perhaps you have been looking for someone to blame. If the person on the receiving end is a real person known to you, the dream is pointing out that you have probably been treating them unfairly in some way. Dreams are rarely concerned with blaming someone else: take it as a hint to 'consider the beam in thine own eye' – it may turn out to be yourself who deserves the criticism!

If you dream that someone is accusing you

There is likely to be a strong element of personal guilt hidden inside a dream in which someone is making an allegation about you. If the dream is of a real life situation involving real life people, of course you will recognize the fact. If not, it could be your own guilty conscience at work. The real cause for an accusation will probably be encrypted in the dream, and will need unscrambling through your own *Association of ideas.*

See also: ABUSE

ACNE *Your complexion has become unsightly*

If dream pimples mark your face

Your complexion or the condition of your skin often symbolise your habitual way of expressing your *Persona* – the image of yourself that you want others to see and accept. Acne on your face means that your faults are on the surface, and obvious to others.

If dream acne affects a part of the body normally kept covered

The implication is that you are keeping some unsavoury truth about yourself a secret from others (a common enough situation in real life) and feeling worried lest it be discovered. There may of course be an actual medical reason which is causing you anxiety and coming to the surface in your dream life.

See also: CLOTHES; NAKED

THE KEY TO DREAM ANALYSIS

ACROBATICS   *Possessing amazing agility*

When you dream that someone else is the acrobat

We might say that someone is 'bending over backwards' to do something, meaning that they are going to great lengths, usually to do someone a favour or accommodate their needs. We might say that someone could do something or other 'standing on their head', meaning that they find the task easy. When someone you know seems in the dream to have become an acrobat, they may have been doing you a favour in real life. But more likely it will mean that you or they have made the best of a situation and performed a symbolic somersault to find a more secure foothold in life – a better job, perhaps, or a more rewarding position in society.

When you dream that you are performing athletic feats

Your own *Inner feelings* are showing you that the inner self is not bound by the usual laws of materiality or gravity, being unencumbered by the physical body. Note any other features of the dream carefully, for dreams of this nature usually carry a powerful and very personal message.

See also: AGILITY

Acting out your dreams

If you are exchanging notes with other like-minded people who want to find out more about their dreams and thence their own selves, you can organize a little dramatic play based on one of your more complicated dreams which involve social relationships – a re-enactment with real people representing the characters in your dream. Role playing such as this will often help to clarify obscure issues and indicate factors you would otherwise have missed. It may help you to identify any *Trigger events* in your everyday life which may have prompted the dream. Their suggestions may well prove useful, but try not to let your friends and associates interpret your dream for you: only you can do that fully and successfully.

See also: Relationship dreams; Sharing your dreams

THE KEY TO DREAM ANALYSIS

Active and passive roles

In your dream you may be taking part in the action, or you may simply be an onlooker as events unfold in your sleeping awareness. When we first take note of our dreams and begin recording them, our dreaming role tends to be passive. As our understanding of dreams increases, so our own participation in the dreams tends to become more and more active. To some extent this reflects our character in real life – not physically, but at the level of our thought processes. The more active we become in our dreams, the more imaginatively constructive our minds become during waking hours, It follows that the act of recording your dreams can have a positive effect on the type of person you are!

ACTORS   *Putting on a performance*

If you are the one doing the acting

The implication of this dream is that you have not been altogether honest in your real life relationships. Of course there are many reasons which compel us to modify our behaviour which are not necessarily dishonest; but this dream is suggesting that you are not altogether happy with this particular deception.

If others are doing the acting

The same principle applies: either you have seen through someone else's little deception, or the dream may be warning you to beware of insincerity on someone's part. If you know the dream actors in your personal life, the meaning of the dream will probably be fairly obvious to you; but a dream involving anonymous actors performing may be implying that someone with whom you are associated will prove unreliable.

If the actors you see in the dream are real, recognizable actors

They may be characters perhaps from a favourite TV show, or a film if this has a definite meaning for you. In this case the presence of real actors in your dream underlines the feelings you have for them. If, for instance, you feel that a certain TV soap is typical of normal, everyday life, and if your dream features characters from that series, they will be setting the dream-scene for you as a normal, everyday situation. But if they are from a show or a film that you thought spiteful or unpleasant in some way, then that kind of behaviour will be the context of your dream. Always remember your own feelings – your *Theme mood* – with regard to these dream figures: they will provide the clue.

See also: THEATRE

Adlerian dreams

As opposed to Freudian and Jungian dreams, Adlerian dreams are orientated towards power, or the sense of striving after power – or equally, towards an awareness of weakness and the absence of power. Alfred Adler (1870-1937) was a colleague of Freud, and it was he who introduced the concept of the inferiority complex. He pointed out that children during the first few years of life, being small and weak and ignorant about the ways of the world, are bound to suffer from feelings of inadequacy. The resultant sense of inferiority he saw as the root of neurosis, and the chief trigger for many of our dreams. He argued that an individual is bound to look for ways to redress the power balance, whether consciously or unconsciously, if not through their patterns of behaviour while awake, at least through their imagination by way of dreams. Dreams, he maintained, can form a source of emotional compensation, rehearsing ways to assert power in one form or another. Dreams which include a feeling of helplessness, or of trying to gain access to a more secure place, or of dominating or bullying other people, or of being in command – these are typical Adlerian dreams. They are allied to the *Plant-nature dreams* included in the concept of the *World dream*, in which, as a step above the 'mineral-nature' of the world, they can be seen as representing a psychic leap forward from the usual dreams of everyday relationships and material ambitions.

See also: *Helplessness; Power orientation*

THE KEY TO DREAM ANALYSIS

ADVERSARY   *A mysterious, threatening character*

This dream character is likely to be one of the *Archetypes of the unconscious mind,* but it can sometimes be identified as the *Personal shadow* itself. The adversary represents any major factor that you have not been facing up to in waking life, and by ignoring it you have allowed it to build itself up in your subconscious mind until it has assumed menacing proportions. Any specific worry or temporary difficulty that has not been dealt with by your conscious mind may appear in dreams as an *Assailant* rather than an adversary, which has a more permanent nature. Try to face up to the image and identify it: the dream itself should provide the clue. Though menacing, it cannot really harm you, as it is probably already a part of your own psyche. However, an aggressive or threatening figure in your dream, whether a person or an animal, may carry some kind of identifying feature that will enable you to place it in terms of your work, your relationships, your recreation, or your family life. If you can put a name to this cryptic fear, you will be better able to deal with it.

See also: ASSAILANT; DEMON; OPPONENT; XENOPHOBIA

ADVICE   *Handing over helpful information*

If you dream you are being given advice by someone you know

If the adviser is a reliable sort of person known to you personally, you will probably be able to relate the dream incident to an incident in waking life, and understand what the dream is trying to tell you. It will certainly be a personal matter that only you can interpret successfully.

If you are being advised by an unknown wise person

Though this friendly figure is not known to you in real life, it may in fact be a part of your own self – an *Archetype of the unconscious mind.* In this case you would do well to heed their advice. because it will certainly be of great value to you. It is your own best advice to yourself!

THE KEY TO DREAM ANALYSIS

If you dream you are giving advice to someone else

The dream could be warning you not to interfere where you are not wanted. Note who you are giving the advice too, and how does that person react? Your dream advice, of course, is not necessarily *bad* advice, but never jump to conclusions; think it over and look at these various possibilities objectively and thoroughly.

See also: GODDESS; KING; QUEEN; WISE PERSON

Affection (A theme mood)

If the contents of your dream call for a mood of affection: a pleasant dream of family and friends, perhaps, this is merely reflecting your own waking feelings. Sometimes, however, you may experience this feeling during the dream or after you wake, when the subject matter of the dream has been far from pleasant. To dream of feeling affection for something you or other people may find repugnant in waking life is a clear warning that you are harbouring or hanging on to some features or characteristics which set you at odds with other people, and which you would be better off without.

Aggression (A theme mood)

In a dream the feeling of aggression tends to suggest a psychic imbalance or an unrealistic conflict on the part of the dreamer. The first part of a complicated dream may have aggression as its theme; the second part perhaps may display a feeling of reconciliation or contentment. If the feeling of aggression persists, it may be pointing to feelings of guilt in the dreamer. Aggression in real life is also a way of discouraging an unwanted person or their unwelcome advances; in the language of dreams the mood points to something, some characteristic, that the dreamer does not want to face up to in waking life.

See also: ANGER; *Arrogance; Hate*

AGILITY   *Unusual physical abilities*

If you are performing amazing contortions in your dream

The *Inner feelings,* also known as the higher emotional centre, and which supplies your dream images, are not bound by physical laws, or even by the *thought* of physical laws. In dreams, unencumbered by your sleeping body, you can defy the force of gravity! This can be very encouraging, but it can have a negative side: the dream may be pointing out that you have been evading your responsibilities or are hiding some truth which would be better released. By dancing in the air you may be hurting someone's feelings in real life, and this can do more harm than you might at first think.

If you dream that someone else known to you is performing physical feats

Perhaps you have been trying to pin this person down in some way, and are finding it very difficult. They seem to have an unfair advantage perhaps, or an enviable ability to succeed where you are floundering. This is a reflection of your own feelings rather than the feelings of this other person who probably does not want to become involved.

See also: ACROBATICS

ALTAR   *A sacred place*

If you are merely observing an altar in your dream

Whether you are a religious person or not, an altar represents the centre of worship and devotion within your feelings – the place that you would not want to see defiled with anything you normally dissociate from that feeling of special importance. Different people have differing principles, and will be devoted to different things, but at the heart of everyone's feelings, symbolically, is the table of the altar, the holy of holies. It may be associated with the feelings you have for another person. Perhaps you feel that your relationship is not openly acceptable for some reason, and you would like to make it so.

THE KEY TO DREAM ANALYSIS

If you are placing something on the altar in your dream

If you can identify the object you have placed there, it is sure to have great significance for you, and, as usual, only you can interpret the dream fully. If you are not sure what the object was, think round it very carefully, using your *Association of ideas*. Remember too if anything else was already on the altar, for this may offer a clue. Remember that the symbol of an altar may represent either a principle which you already consider to be beyond reproach, or a circumstance that you would dearly like to make acceptable and free from feelings of guilt.

See also: ABBEY; CATHEDRAL; CHURCH

Amusement (A theme mood)

Amusement often features in *Children's dreams*. In the case of most adults, however, a genuine feeling of amusement is rather unusual in a dream, because the function of dreams is to instruct rather than entertain. It may, however, occur during a *Balancing dream* pointing out that you have been taking some situation or incident too seriously. Real amusement is more likely to feature in a *Wish fulfilment dream*, or a *Lucid dream* in which the dreamer is actually manipulating the dream events.

See also: Laughter

Analysing dreams

The first essential step for dream analysis has to be: remember it and write it down complete with all its details, taking care not to exaggerate any part of it to make it more interesting or pleasing to your own ego. See the section on *Recording dreams*. It is often best to keep your dream-notes private, because there is always the temptation to make it sound better, or to put yourself in a better light, or perhaps to modify parts of it relating to family members. Your notes must be honest if you are to understand the dream and benefit from it. Look on your dream as a story with a general theme, a plot, a storyline and a conclusion. Write down everything in sequence, and then read between the lines. Try to remember the emotions you may have felt as the dream unfolded: they will be very significant. Good stories usually have more than one meaning, a 'story within the story'. Your dream may have any number of meanings hidden in it, and the deeper you go, the more important the information you find. Your own unconscious mind is expert at using symbols, and virtually everything that happens within your dream is a symbol. Symbols can have more than one meaning, and you will of course refer to the entries in this book to help bring out what they mean to you. Anyone can analyse a dream on its surface, but only the dreamer can interpret it fully. Only the dreamer knows all the events and experiences upon which the dream is based. Think it all through very thoroughly. Think round everything that featured in the dream, as far as you can remember, exploring every possible meaning – particularly if these thoughts make you feel uncomfortable. That means you are approaching something your sense of pride is trying to keep hidden, and you would be better off exposing it to *your own* gaze. After all, the first rule for understanding divine truth is to 'know thyself'!

ANGEL *A supernatural being*

The concept of the *World dream* explains how the angel-principle should be regarded in relation to our everyday world. Within the human psyche angels comprise the antithesis of the aggressive 'plant-nature' and the competitive, often sex-obsessed 'animal nature' in ourselves. As dream symbols, angels serve to balance the world of nature; their presence acts as a counterbalance to both *Freudian dreams* and *Adlerian dreams*. Precisely what an angel means for you will depend almost entirely on your own experiences in life, your own ideas of what if anything constitutes 'an angel' and what you suppose the function of an angel to be. In most cultures they are thought of as divine messengers, and made of light. When their dream image is drawn from the *Collective unconscious* they are able to represent whatever the will of God is perceived to be by the individual, in any given set of circumstances.

THE KEY TO DREAM ANALYSIS

If you dream of an angel, and this is a good experience

In the West, it is usual to think of angels as gentle beings who might be relied upon to give a helping hand when it is most needed: loving, forgiving, sexless and impartial. If your dream angel appeared to typical western form, winged, robed and filled with love, the message it conveys will be one of reassurance, condolence and possibly gentle reproof.

If meeting your dream angel was a bad experience

In some countries, especially in the East, angels are thought of in an unsentimental way as divine administrators, doling out judgment, punishment or reward as it may be deserved. They may be seen as fierce masculine beings wielding a sword or battleaxe. If your dream angel was like this, you can be sure that it was bearing a message: one that you do not want to listen to in waking life. Try to fathom out what this message is, because it is certain to be an important matter of conscience. If an angel appears before you in a *Dawn dream*, you should be in no doubt about the message: it will be for you alone.

See also: JUDGE

ANGER *(This can also be a theme mood)*

If you are the angry one in the dream

Dream anger is often expressed when someone during the day has drawn attention to a personal characteristic that you are sensitive about and may be acting as a barrier to your peace of mind. They may have done this quite unconsciously, provoking a defensive response by hinting at this flaw in your character. The idea of 'righteous indignation' sounds reasonable – the other person seems to be in the wrong if you feel upset about something they said or did; but justifiable anger seldom happens in the dream world. Dream anger usually suggests that something is psychologically wrong – something that ought to be put right.

THE KEY TO DREAM ANALYSIS

If someone else is the angry one

Anger can sometimes actually be seen in a dream, like a dark cloud issuing from the angry character's mouth; sometimes it can be smelled as a rotten-plant smell. A dream of this nature may be purely informative if your own well-being has been compromised.But sometimes the emotion becomes transferred during a dream, so that the person who triggered your own anger appears to be the angry one instead. In either case, dream anger is likely to imply that your *Inner feelings* know that a change of attitude is needed on your part, but your thoughts and everyday emotions are unwilling to face up to this in waking life. Dreams featuring anger call for personal interpretation by thinking round each incident in the dream sequence and trying to identify any mental or emotional barriers. They are sure to exist, and you would be better off without them.

See *also:* ABUSE; ACCUSATIONS; *Aggression;Plant-nature dreams*

Animal-nature dreams

A dream classification based on the *World dream*, and related to *Freudian dreams* in that the sexual impulse usually has a part to play. When a dream, which does not seem to reflect any incident or attitude in everyday life, involves competition with others in matters of boundaries, territory or morality, it can be said to be an animal-nature dream, based on deep-seated instincts common to us all.

ANIMALS   *Any living non-human creatures*

If you seem to have become an animal in your dream

A dream like this may be an interesting reflection of the *World dream*, or it may even be a *Reincarnation dream*. Very often, though, the dreamer may have been wondering or imagining what it would be like to be an animal of this sort, and the dream is granting your wish to find out. Or perhaps your own attitude in your waking life has been very much like the instinctive behaviour of the animal in your dream. More information about this possibility can be found under the headings *Controlling dreams, Encouraging dreams, Incubating dreams,* and *Volitional dreams.*

THE KEY TO DREAM ANALYSIS

If animals feature in your dream

Somebody like a farmer or perhaps a zoo-keeper, or a pet-owner, to whom certain animals are particularly familiar, is likely to find them included as a background feature in a dream, merely to set the scene in familiar surroundings. But where this is obviously not the case, and animals have featured strongly in a *Personal dream*, personal interpretation will be needed. Heavy, horned animals, usually bulls, are particularly significant, and carry with them the idea of powerful masculinity best not disturbed. As a simple warning, or perhaps to reflect an anxiety already present in the dreamer's mind, their appearance may suggest that the dreamer should take care not to upset the kind of man who may fit this category in real life. A shy forest animal such as a startled deer among the trees may be telling you that somebody close to you, or you yourself, have been evading your social obligations and taking refuge instead in the 'forest of the mind'. If a person close to you in waking life has been behaving like a particular type of animal – perhaps greedy like a pig, or cruel and fierce like a wolf, or liable to charge blindly like a bull, or rampage like a rhinoceros – they may well assume this animal guise in your dream.

If you dream of your pet animals

The dream may be offering a practical message about your pets, and some people have gleaned useful information in this way. But sometimes the *Personal shadow* can take the form of a fierce animal, and when it does so this dream animal is often a travesty or distortion of a domestic pet familiar to the dreamer. Sometimes it becomes a terrifying *Nightmare*, but it is a fairly common dream occurrence which draws attention to the fact that this apparently demonic creature represents something that is actually very close and familiar – a part of the dreamer's own psyche which has built itself up into this frightening form within the subconscious mind. It could be a stern warning against following occult practices.

See also: Animal-nature dreams; BIRDS; BULL;
COCKEREL; DEMON; DOG; COW; EAGLE;
ELEPHANT; HORSE; PARROT; PIG; WOLF; ZOO

THE KEY TO DREAM ANALYSIS

ANTIQUE   *Something very old and valuable*

The *Collective unconscious* includes contents that probably date back many thousands of years to the dawn of human awareness, and this vast psychological sea is the most likely source of an antique that features in your dream. This is all the more probable if the dream is a particularly vivid one – and even more so if it comes to you as a *Dawn dream*.

If someone known to you shows or gives you an antique in your dream

You can be certain that this person is in possession of, or is offering you, something of great spiritual benefit. They want to share with you a secret, a desire, or a practical quality that you would be unwise to reject. Purely on a psychological basis – that is, without a potentially spiritual content – the antique could represent sexual impulses or a hoped-for sexual relationship. In mystical terms, while the sexual element is not precluded, the dream may be pointing to a spiritual path now open to you.

If no-one else is involved in this dream of an antique

The dream object represents something, or some abstract quality, that is very precious to you: something rooted in the past that affects you strongly, and which you do not feel able to express in more realistic terms. The dream object may be a chest, or a casket, or a cupboard, or some other container, and in this case you can be sure that it contains something of great value or lasting significance. In mythology, Pandora's box contained all the passions and problems of the world, which escaped when it was opened, leaving only hope in the box. This is usually seen as a symbol of marriage with all its ups and downs, blessings and frustrations. The dream antique is very much a personal symbol, and only the dreamer will be able to think round all the implications and possibilities connected with it, and reach a satisfactory conclusion.

See also: ARCHAEOLOGY; VASE

Apprehension   (A theme mood)

A very commonly experienced dream emotion that relates to an unsolved problem or deep-seated worry. Feelings of apprehension or *Doubt* during the course of a dream are liable to change to *Relief* or *Reassurance*, indicating that a solution to whatever is troubling the dreamer is being suggested. Feelings of this nature are typical of *Lost* dreams, and reflect any anxieties which may be hidden deep within the dreamer's psyche.

ARCHAEOLOGY   *Digging up secrets from the past*

If ancient artefacts are being dug from the ground

Anything in your dream that is being revealed from its ancient hiding place, or anything that seems on the point of being revealed, is likely to represent some piece of information or new understanding coming to conscious awareness. In effect, you have been digging into the depths of your own *Personal unconscious*. The implication of this dream is that this knowledge has been hidden for a very long time; it may even represent something inherited from your ancestors – a family secret which should now be revealed to you. Whatever it is, it is likely to have psychological significance, though it may have no material value. Only you, the dreamer, can discover the true meaning.

If an ancient corpse or skeleton is being exhumed

This could be the symbol of some factor, some idea, some principle, long gone and forgotten, that is now being revived. You may well feel that it should be allowed to remain forgotten. But it can also signify the 'bones' of a new idea based on ancient understanding – an idea that may have useful potential.

See also: ANTIQUE; BONES; PIT; SKELETON

THE KEY TO DREAM ANALYSIS

Archetypes of the collective unconscious

The concept of the archetype was formulated by the famous pioneer psychiatrist Professor Jung, and expressed in his system of analytical psychology. Jung could see a tendency common to all people, to understand and regulate their lives in a way conditioned by the whole previous history of mankind. This tendency involved a series of shared experiences which grouped various aspects of their collective psyche into recognizable forms intuitively understood. These primordial images remained basically constant, though in their form and detail they could vary widely to suit the individual's understanding and cultural background. These subtle manifestations of intuitive perception rose to awareness and made their presence known – often by way of dreams – usually at times of exceptional importance, when something momentous or awe-inspiring was taking place, and in particular if a change came about or was due to come about in the individual's psychological orientation.

Whether we call them 'bundles of psychic energy', or emotional constants on which people pin their faith, these archetypal images still rise to our awareness to warn, or advise, or admonish, or reassure us. When this happens, we usually feel duty-bound to take heed of their messages. They leave a lasting impression on our minds, so that we are left in no doubt as to their psychic reality, their sincerity of purpose. Though they usually remain below our surface of awareness, they could be called collectively the highest part, the pinnacle, of our own individual selfhood. Because they are shared in common with the rest of humanity and originate from the sum total of human history, in the advice they offer they carry the strength and weight of all human wisdom and experience.

The most commonly experienced archetypes include: the _Self,_ often visualized as an innocent child experiencing the world and observing our every move, watching that we do not act in a way harmful to ourselves; in men there is the *anima,* and in women the *animus,* representing the feminine element within a man which enables him to understand and relate to women, and the male element within a woman which gives her an intuitive understanding of men and their needs. In both men and women there is the archetype of the

Wise person, available to offer good advice in times of stress; the *Hero* or heroine; and the *Personal shadow* which occupies the darkest part of our own *Personal unconscious* mind. There is the *Persona*, which indicates the 'face' we like to present to the world for our own self-preservation. Though primordial and archetypal, the form and function of all these stems directly from our own life experiences, and can give us valuable information about ourselves when we heed their message.

Arrogance   (A theme mood)

A thoroughly unpleasant emotion, either when awake or when dreaming. The dream in which arrogance is the over-riding theme may reflect a mistake attitude adopted by the dreamer in waking life. You may not be an arrogant person, but the dream is telling you that you need to cultivate more self-confidence, that you suffer from unnecessary feelings of inferiority in your everyday dealings with others. Such feelings often feature in *Plant-nature dreams,* or *Adlerian dreams* orientated towards the pursuit of power, which amounts to much the same thing as habitually feeling inferior. Dreams of this type need analysing very thoughtfully.

ART   *The creation of pleasing images*

If you are an artist in your dream

It may be that you are in fact an artist, and creating artwork is typical of your everyday life, in which case the dream-sequence is merely setting the scene for the rest of the dream as an everyday affair. But if art does not normally play a part in your life, the dream plainly shows that some sort of creative work is being done or planned: something is being prepared perhaps for public viewing. The inspiration for your artwork is likely to arise from your own personality, and represents an aspect of yourself that you feel shows you in a good light. It could also mean that you are trying to show some object or situation in a better light by falsifying the details, or presenting a somewhat exaggerated view.

THE KEY TO DREAM ANALYSIS

If you are watching an artist at work in your dream

Unless the artist is a person known to you in real life, he or she could be one of the *Archetypes of the unconscious mind* making a point for your information. It may be the *Persona*, painting a sweetened view of your best profile. The dream suggests that you are falsifying your position in some way not altogether pleasing to your conscience. If the painter is a real acquaintance, the likelihood is that they are the one presenting the 'prettied-up' view, and trying to pull the wool over your eyes.

See also: PAINTING

ASSAILANT *An unknown dream-enemy or opponent*

One of the *Archetypes of the unconscious mind*, the assailant is a dream figure representing matters which the dreamer has found upsetting or challenging, and has not been able to deal with during waking hours. Perhaps you have been hoping that some problem will go away by ignoring it, but when they are psychologically based such things do not go away permanently: they are pushed into your unconscious mind, to be dealt with by the *Inner feelings*. If there is still no satisfactory conclusion they are liable to become absorbed by the *Personal shadow*. A dream assailant is broadly similar to the archetype of the *Adversary*, but tends to represent a one-off circumstance, something from outside oneself. A dream adversary relates to a permanent predicament – a long-term condition existing within the psyche. The actual nature of your assailant will probably be obscure in the dream, and it may simply be felt as an unseen, threatening presence. If you can practice *Re-entering a dream*, you may be better placed to identify the problem, and the dream itself may offer a solution. If not, analyse the dream carefully by thinking round every detail, noting your emotions at every stage, and listing any associated ideas and themes – especially if you find them vaguely upsetting: these may hold the clue!

See also: ADVERSARY; OPPONENT

THE KEY TO DREAM ANALYSIS

Association of ideas

When you are feeling baffled by a dream, it is a good idea to make a list of all the elements of the dream, setting them out in sequence. Then, by following your own train of thought, your own association of ideas, write down in turn everything else that comes to mind, everything the dream details remind you of: happenings, characters, emotions and themes, associations past and present. Write them down as though following a storyline for each item, every new idea you come up with suggesting its own sequence of possible events, its own new train of thought, and continue until you run out of ideas. If you feel that any particular train of thought is becoming unpleasant, something you would rather not pursue – pursue it just the same: you could be approaching something very significant that your everyday mind is trying to keep hidden, and this could be the whole crux of the dream. It is helpful too if you make out a *Dream questionnaire*, and perhaps turn the dream and your thoughts about it into an organized *Dream diagram*, showing each connection in turn until you reach a considered conclusion.

See also: *Free association*

AUTUMN   *Past the prime*

This is quite a common dream metaphor: the fall of the year marks the end of warm sunshine, flowers and greenery. Plant life at least is drawing to a close, or approaching its season of dormancy in a brief spectacle of colour. A poetic comparison with the 'autumn of our years' has always been compelling, and when autumn features in your dream this is its probable significance. Perhaps you are feeling no longer young, and looking forward – with eagerness, or resignation, or perhaps trepidation – to your own declining years. But the symbol may not be referring to the dreamer's age: to dream you are walking through a forest with falling leaves usually suggests that an easy phase of your life has passed its climax and is approaching full cycle. It may not be a bad thing. Look on it as a quiet season when you can take stock for the future, perhaps no more than a resting period until the time for spring regrowth.

See also: CLOCK; FOREST

B

BABY *A very young child*

The innocent child *Self* is a major *Archetype of the unconscious mind* and expresses the essence of the individual, the basic self without all its habits and hang-ups, without having been influenced by the world around it, without what some would call 'character' or 'personality'. A blank sheet, in effect, upon which all the varying impressions of the world are recorded as life goes on.

If you dream of a very young or new-born baby

This is most likely to symbolise any new creation or new idea that has come to light – a new enterprise, a new career, a new understanding, or a new way of looking at a familiar situation. A baby is innocent, naive, 'silly' in the original sense of the word. The dream may be pointing out your own reactions to some completely unfamiliar set of circumstances. Suppose you move to a strange country, or join a group of people with unfamiliar ideas, you may feel a bit 'silly', and the dream will be reflecting your own inner feelings. But, as always, there may be a more straightforward and obvious meaning to the dream symbol – you may have been thinking a lot about babies for whatever reason – or it may be referring to a real baby known to you, and it should then be interpreted as a *Personal dream.*

See also: CHILD

Balancing dreams

The dreaming process works naturally in the long-term to bring about a balanced personality, levelling out extremes. In a completely balanced personality, for instance, one's feelings for others will be balanced by one's feelings for oneself, though these may range between the extremes of love and hate. The attitudes we apply to ourselves *should* be applied to others in equal measure, and dreams often point out the somewhat inevitable discrepancies in this respect. Balance works in other ways too: some people may go through life peacefully and unadventurously, never acting in an unkind or aggressive manner – but their dreams may sometimes seem full of daring exploits and involve an alarming degree of violence and passion. The opposite type of people who seem to live constantly on the edge of their nerves, hyperactive perhaps, quick to pick a quarrel or fly into a rage, may experience dreams of gentle pursuits, peace and harmony. A well-balanced person is not necessarily a *good* person in the usually-accepted sense of the word, though morals feature prominently in balancing dreams: over-virtuous people frequently dream of behaving in a thoroughly immoral manner, while at the other extreme an undisciplined person who cares little for the rights of others may dream of discipline, morality and justice. Striking a balance within the cycle of the mind – giving and taking, conscious and unconscious – is a basic function of the *Inner feelings* finding expression by way of the dreaming self. Religious feelings too, or a lack of appreciation of spiritual matters, these are often balanced out in dreams that may appear baffling – dreams which, it seems, are intended to stretch the dreamer's creative imagine.

BALL *A solid sphere*

You may of course be a fan, or an expert at some ball game, and your dreams may well reflect this – only you can know. But a ball can be a highly significant dream symbol. *Wholeness* can be symbolised by a sphere or a ball, and if you are consciously working towards this psychological and spiritual goal, the *Self* may well be featured as a ball that is aimed at the goal.

If you dream that you see a ball bouncing or rolling

This symbol can imply that you are finding yourself at odds with the rest of society, or with your own community. Ball games such as football and baseball are hugely popular, of course, and it often seems that the crowd in a stadium are totally at unison, totally orientated towards some 'goal', all acting as one. Opposing sides and their supporters will be a mirror image of the other side, and their orientation is equally single-minded. This could be what your dream is telling you. The ball is the neutral odd one out in the game, and this could apply to you, in the game of life.

THE KEY TO DREAM ANALYSIS

If you dream that you are bouncing the ball yourself

This reflects the feeling that you are in complete harmony with your own particular surroundings and the people around you: you are at ease with yourself and with your relationships. However, the dream may be implying that you have been ignoring the needs of some minority group, or that you have become too partisan in your commitments. It could be an important symbol warning you to take stock of your attitude to others with whom you come in contact.

See also: Spherical symbolisation of the self

BALLET *Graceful physical conformity*

If you have only recently started taking an interest in your dreams, when you dream of ballet dancers you will probably merely be watching them perform. If your dream studies are fairly well advanced, however, you will very likely be taking part in the dance yourself. In either case it will have a personal significance. In effect, ballet is the art of telling a story set to music, by way of graceful physical movements. Poise and confidence both play a large part, and ballet training must involve a great deal of strain and suffering before the dancers get it right. Ballet can perhaps become obsessive, for the true feelings of the performers have to remain subdued or hidden: everyone has to follow the correct routine. If you know the dream dancers in real life – not necessarily as dancers but as your everyday friends and colleagues – the dream may be demonstrating your admiration for their expertise in whatever they normally do. The dream is expressing your own deep emotions, and your mood during the dream or shortly after waking may be important as a pointer. Ballet dancers, in effect, are wearing a disguise, and this may suggest that deception of some sort is taking place. The dream may be expressing your own sorrow or sense of resignation or guilt at being forced to 'play a part' in life, never free to follow your conscience or your own preferences.

See also: ACTING; DANCE; THEATRE

BALLOON   *A free-floating sphere*

If you dream of a mysterious balloon

A bubble-like sphere floating over the earth is a fair description of the nature of your own *Inner feelings*. Unaffected by the force of gravity, and unrestricted even by your physical body, the inner feelings are able to float free: the spiritual side of your nature can rise above earthly cares and problems. This dream could be an invitation to look for a more spiritual path through life – and to practice recording and understanding your dreams is an excellent way to start.

If you dream of a children's balloon

The symbol will be reflecting the carefree feelings of innocence normally associated with party balloons. Balloons of this sort suggest material enjoyment, either innocent or not-so-innocent, and may be indicating a real situation of which you are well aware. If other people who are known to you in real life appear in the dream, their pleasure-seeking ways may be heading for a setback. But if no other recognizable person features in your dream, it could be a gentle warning that all good things must come to an end: your balloon may burst at any time. Whatever situation you are currently putting your trust in does not seem to have a reliable future.

If you dream of a hot-air balloon

A passenger-carrying balloon can have a similar meaning to either of the above alternatives: the context of the dream should make the symbol clear. The implication is that the passengers are being raised above the common run of humanity; they are being lifted by heat – and the dream-source of heat is usually the passions – the intensity of people's outward feelings. But man-made balloons have to land sooner or later, and passions are liable to change. There is an element of desire or wishful thinking about this dream – the wish that you could really float above the world and its problems.

See also: BALL; FLYING; *Spherical symbolisation of self*

BAMBOO *Symbol of flexibility*

Like the willow, as a universally understood symbol, bamboo expresses the propensity to yield to a more powerful force, to bend before the hurricane. The stoutest tree may be uprooted or broken off in a gale, but the bamboo, whilst green and growing, though bent double, will spring up again unharmed. The application to circumstances in waking life is likely to be obvious: it is better to yield to whatever powerful force cannot be controlled or resisted, rather than risk destruction. As a warning dream, the image of bamboo bending in the wind could be telling you not to fight against unreasonable odds, whatever the real-life situation may be: find a way to let the troubles pass safely over your head. If the real-life situation is not clear to you, try to remember if anyone or anything else featured in your dream, for they may provide the clue. You, yourself, are probably the 'bamboo', but you may still need to identify the 'gale'. Or perhaps you, yourself, may be represented by the hurricane, in which case it is the bamboo that will need identifying. Without malicious intent, you could be hurting someone else's feelings.

See also: AGILITY; BULLYING; HURRICANE; *Submission*

BARN *A storage building*

There is always the possibility that your dream is of a *real* solid barn in a real situation, with a personal meaning for you. But more frequently a dream barn symbolises the *Self*, and in particular, perhaps, that part of the self that you are not normally aware of – the *Personal unconscious mind* and its contents. This image is being presented by your own *Inner feelings*, probably in the light of recent real-life occurrences, so it is likely to carry a strong personal message.

If you dream that the barn is empty

Emptiness is the feeling that the dream is portraying: you may have been feeling that your life is empty, or meaningless, or worthless. Your barn should be full of contents, even if they are only your hopes and fears, and if you dream of the barn again, it may well seem to have become miraculously filled with valuable possessions. The inner feelings often present a white lie intended to set your mind on a different and more positive track.

If you dream that someone is in the barn

This dream character may seem harmless, or perhaps mysterious and threatening. Unless of course it is a real person known to you in waking life, this mysterious figure is an image arisen from the unconscious mind. A dream such as this implies that you have been pushing some problem aside rather than facing up to it in waking life. It may be a long-term problem, a repressed memory or psychological block that is affecting your peace of mind. Or it may be a short-term challenge, some problem that has arisen recently and which is worrying you. It may even be your own *Shadow*, composed of some of your own characteristics which you want no-one – not even yourself – to know about. Remember that it is your own dream barn, so take some trouble to think round each dream feature very carefully, and arrive at an honest interpretation.

See also: ADVERSARY; ASSAILANT; HUT; STORE

BATTLE   *Group aggression*

Occasionally, personal aggression or taking part in a battle is a feature of a *Balancing dream* that may perhaps be compensating for an unusually gentle lifestyle, and equally you may dream of attacking people as a way of compensating for an overly defensive attitude in daily life. But as a rule attacking someone or defending yourself in a dream tends symbolically to reflect your current situation in everyday life. You may have been feeling that everyone is against you: it is a common experience to feel that you are the odd one out, or under siege, and fearing that your position is being undermined by the actions of others. People can become paranoid if they feel they are being persecuted – and of course such a feeling may well turn out to be justified. Life often seems like a battlefield too when you are simply trying to improve your lot in the material sphere. In general, dreams of aggression call for anappraisal of your own lifestyle: your dream battle may be warning you against selfish or hurtful behaviour. Remember that the cycle of tit-for-tat is only likely to be broken by modifying your own attitude – bearing in mind not only the immediate benefit, but long-term relationships too.

See also: *Aggression;* ANGER

BATTLEMENTS   *Security against assault*

Security is the key-word where this dream symbol is concerned, but security for a definite reason – either you or someone else in the dream is under threat. This may be your situation in waking life: you feel the need to defend yourself, and this may seem well justified. But the assault is liable to increase while you cower behind your dream battlements. Similarly if some other person is finding safety against your own attacks: there will be a genuine reason for the dream, and you should come to a conclusion about the wisdom of pursuing your current course in life.

See also: BATTLE; FORTRESS; TOWER

Biblical dreams

There are many accounts of visions or waking inspirations in the Bible, culminating in the Revelation of John the Divine; but few of dreams. In the New Testament dreams are given short shrift. An angel is said to have appeared to Joseph in a dream to explain the extraordinary circumstance of his wife Mary's pregnancy (*Matthew 1)*, and the three wise men were reportedly warned in a dream not to return to Herod after visiting the newborn Jesus (*Matthew 2)*. Apart from these, no dreams were recorded, though such prophetic dreams were plainly treated with respect. The Old Testament has:

The barley cake (Judges, 7)

This was the Midian soldier's dream of a 'stale barley cake' which rolled into their camp and flattened a tent. He recounted the dream to a fellow soldier, who remarked that it predicted their defeat at the hands of Gideon's forces (Gideon himself happened to overhear this as he reconnoitred the enemy positions under cover of darkness). Following this somewhat unlikely event Gideon immediately mustered his forces and attacked and defeated the Midianites, though greatly outnumbered. The symbolism of the barley cake may have involved a play on words, the words for 'barley cake' and the name 'Gideon' or his surname 'Jerubbaal' sounding similar; but the more usual explanation lies in the historical situation. Gideon's people lived in the hilly regions where barley was grown, and the barley cake or loaf was one of their basics – a poor quality bread inferior to that baked from wheat flour. The Midianites were a marauding tribe from the plains, used to plundering much of their needs from other more settled tribes. To them, the 'barley-bread people' of the hills were held somewhat in scorn. The idea of their tents flattened by a barley cake carried with it the idea of humiliating defeat at the hands of the hill tribes.

Solomon's visitation (First Book of Kings, 3)

The young, newly appointed King Solomon is reported to have dreamed that he was visited by God, who asked him what he wanted most. Solomon asked for the ability to listen patiently to his people's problems and to rule them with justice. His wish was granted, and because he had not asked for selfish things such as wealth, numerous wives and a long life, these things were added as a divine bonus. This account has the ring of a story invented later to explain and justify Solomon's enormous wealth and his reputation for wisdom.

The wheat sheaves bowing down (Genesis, 37)

Joseph, son of Jacob, annoyed his ten brothers by telling them of his dream in which they were all together in a field gathering the harvest, when his brothers' sheaves gathered round and bowed down to Joseph's sheaf. He went on to relate another dream in which the sun, the moon, and eleven stars all bowed down before him. Already jealous because they believed he was their father's favourite son, Joseph's brothers reacted by selling him as a slave to some traders bound for Egypt. Then they stained his 'many-coloured coat' with goat's blood and took this back to their father, claiming that their brother had been killed by a wild animal.

Pharaoh's butler *(Genesis, 40)*

Later, as a slave of the Pharaoh Joseph found himself thrown quite unjustly into prison together with two of Pharaoh's servants, a butler and a baker. They both had dreams which Joseph was able to interpret. In the butler's dream he saw a vine with three branches, which sprouted, blossomed, and produced grapes as he watched. He gathered and pressed the grapes and offered the juice to Pharaoh, who took the cup and drank. Joseph's interpretation of the dream was this: In three days you will be back in Pharaoh's favour and reinstated as his butler (and this is what happened). The vine he saw as the symbol of a good life and plentiful times. The three branches he interpreted as three days, and the fact that the butler had offered all the grapes or their juice to his master and held nothing back for himself showed that he was a faithful and honest servant. The cup Joseph saw as the cup of fate, and the butler had filled it with the good fortune symbolised by the blossoming and fruiting of the vine, and offered it to Pharaoh who accepted it, thus taking back the butler's empty fate and with it his previous denunciation.

Pharaoh's baker *(Genesis, 40)*

The baker dreamed that he was carrying three bread baskets on his head, each filled with fresh produce. The topmost one was piled high with bread and cakes which he was taking to Pharaoh. Suddenly a flock of birds swooped down and ate all the bread and cakes in the topmost basket, and there was nothing the baker could do about it. He was not so fortunate as the butler. The bread and cakes had represented his peace offering to Pharaoh, his begging for pardon, but the ominous birds of fate had robbed him of the chance of reconciliation. This was Joseph's interpretation of the baker's dream: the three baskets represented three days, and after three days the Pharaoh will have the man hanged from a tree, and the birds will feast on his flesh. An upsetting interpretation, but once again the prophecy came true. The baker's best efforts were wasted because

Pharaoh rejected his petition, and his life was forfeit. The grapes had symbolised the butler's life; the bread had represented the baker's life. Raised on high like the topmost basket he was worth no more to Pharaoh than food for the birds. Given the time and place (Egypt around 1700BC) the story could very well be true.

Pharaoh's dream of cows (Genesis, 41)

Many months later Joseph, recommended by the butler, was called upon to interpret Pharaoh's dream, and this is how he related it to Joseph:

In my dream, behold, I stood upon the bank of the river: And behold, there came up out of the river seven kine, fat-fleshed and well favoured: And behold, seven other kine came up after them, poor and very ill favoured and lean-fleshed, such as I never saw in all the land of Egypt for badness: And the lean and ill favoured kine did eat up the first seven fat kine: And when they had eaten them up, it could not be known that they had eaten them; but they were still ill favoured, as at the beginning. So I awoke. Again I slept, and I saw in my dream, and behold, seven ears of wheat came up in one stalk, full and good: And behold, seven ears sprung up after them, withered, thin, and blasted with the east wind: And the thin ears devoured the seven good ears. So I awoke. And I told this unto the magicians; but there was none that could declare it to me.

Joseph saw these two dreams as one, and was able to make the interpretation without hesitation. Egypt depended heavily upon the River Nile, with its annual flooding ensuring good crops for the year. The Egyptian goddess Isis was thought to embody the great river, and it was she in the popular view who sent the annual floods – on her goodwill rested the welfare of the land. Isis was also identified with the cow, a universal symbol of nurture, of motherhood and fertility. Statues and images of her show her wearing the crescent-shaped set of cow horns, and the similarly crescent-shaped half moon was also a favourite symbol. Each cow coming out of the Nile Joseph interpreted as a flood-year – in this case seven fat cows or kine symbolising seven good floods, followed immediately by seven bad ones. The devastating effects of the latter would eat up, or totally cancel out the benefits of the good years preceding them. Ears of wheat were another traditional symbol of Isis. They were also a symbol of Osiris, her consort, brother and husband. As the god of death and resurrection, burial and rebirth, he was closely connected with grain crops, their sowing in the ground and subsequent sprouting and reaping. Joseph's prophecy of seven plentiful years closely followed by seven years of famine was augmented by the second dream: seven good ears of wheat followed and swallowed up by seven bad. The first part of Pharaoh's dream is shown in diagrammatic form in the section on *Dream diagrams*.

Nebuchadnezzar's dream of the idol (Daniel, 2)

After the defeat of Israel during the 6th century BC when the Hebrews were carried off as captives to Chaldea and Babylon, the young intellectual Daniel was among them, and whilst in Babylon he earned his reputation as a teller of dreams for the Babylonian King Nebuchadnezzar II. The Babylonians set much store on dreams and their interpretation, though in a superstitious society like theirs their interpretations now seem dogmatic and obsessed with omens. Most of the recorded dreams from that era were those of kings, and these dreams usually conveyed advice or instructions to build new temples dedicated to various gods or goddesses. Commoners' dreams, judging by the few that have been found recorded on clay tablets, usually involved encounters with shades of the dead, and predicted the imminent death of the dreamer. Inscribed clay tablets were their only permanent records, apart from monumental inscriptions, and the only form of Babylonian literature to have survived, but because of the Hebrew involvement in the Captivity, two of Nebuchadnezzar's dreams found their eventual way into the Hebrew scriptures and the Old Testament. We would probably not have heard of this *Great Dream* of Nebuchadnezzar had he immediately remembered what it had been about, but as soon as he awoke he forgot it. He knew it had been very vivid and plainly important, so he called for his wise men, his advisers, his sorcerers, his magicians and his astrologers, to tell him what the dream had been about, and to interpret it. This was a tall order: the wise men were of course in the dark unless he recalled it and told them what it had been about. The impasse was brought to a head by Nebuchadnezzar, who threatened to have them all killed forthwith. Daniel, having been classed as one of the 'wise men', was in great danger along with the others, Fortunately, that night Daniel had an *Intuitive dream* in which he was shown the king's dream. Next morning he was ushered into the king's presence, and the upshot is that it was Daniel rather than Nebuchadnezzar himself who narrated the dream and simultaneously interpreted it:

Though, O king, sawest, and behold a great image. This great image, whose brightness was excellent, stood before thee; and the form thereof was terrible. This image's head was of fine gold, his breast and his arms of silver, his belly and his thighs of brass, his legs of iron, his feet part of iron and part of clay. Thou sawest till that a stone was cut out without hands, which smote the image upon his feet that were of iron and clay, and brake them to pieces. Then was the iron, the clay, the brass, the silver, and the gold, broken to pieces together, and became like the chaff of the summer threshing floors; and the wind carried them away, that no place was found for them: and the stone that smote the image became a great mountain, and filled the whole earth.

This is the dream; and we will tell the interpretation thereof before the king. Thou, O king, art a king of kings: for the God of heaven hath given thee a kingdom, power, and strength, and glory ... Thou art this head of gold. And after thee shall arise another kingdom inferior to thee, and another third kingdom of brass, which shall bear rule over all the earth. And the fourth kingdom shall be strong as iron: forasmuch as iron breaketh in pieces and subdueth all things: and as iron that breaketh all these, shall it break in pieces and bruise. And whereas thou sawest the feet and toes, part of potter's clay, and part of iron, the kingdom shall be divided: but there shall be in it the strength of the iron, forasmuch as thou sawest the iron mixed with miry clay. And as the toes of the feet were part of iron, and part of clay, so the kingdom shall be partly strong, and partly broken.

Ancient kings were considered living symbols of their kingdoms: when Pharaoh dreamed, his dreams reflected the fate of Egypt; when Nebuchadnezzar dreamed, his dreams reflected the fate of Babylon. Daniel's interpretation of the great image was very much the

Babylonian one rather than a personal interpretation for Nebuchadnezzar alone. The dream image had a head of gold, and certainly Nebuchadnezzar II represented the Golden Age of the Babylonian empire, the period (625–528 BC) commencing with his father Nabopolassar's reign, and continuing until the visionary moving finger at Belshazzar's feast wrote its fateful message on the wall to be interpreted by the then aging Daniel: *Mene mene tekel u-pharsin:* Your kingdom is to be divided between the Medes and Persians. Politically and historically, the 'god with the feet of clay' is usually understood in the following general terms:

Head of gold: The new Babylonian Empire under the rule of Nebuchadnezzar II (fl 600BC);

Chest of silver: The Median/Persian Empire under Cyrus who defeated Babylon (539BC) resulting in the permanent loss of Babylonian independence;

Loins of brass: The Persian Empire under Darius I (c500BC) which further debased Babylonian culture;

Legs of iron: The Greek Empire under Alexander the Great (330BC) who destroyed the remaining Babylonian cities;

Feet of clay: The Roman Empire (c150BC) under which the old Babylonian dynasties died out.

The 'feet of clay' marked the total destruction of Babylon, and indeed, clay is all that remains of the glory that once was the Babylonian Empire. The numerous inscribed clay tablets excavated from the totally flattened ruins are poignant reminders of ancient certainties now long gone. Few empires having flourished so vigorously in their heyday, can have left so little in the way of recognizable remains, or handed down so little to add to our present-day culture.

Daniel was obliged to tread very carefully so as not to offend the king, or annoy him further. His life was still in danger, so he gave the most tactful interpretation. A psychological analysis, though less tactful, would have turned it into a *Personal dream*:

THE KEY TO DREAM ANALYSIS

Head of gold: The king values his own judgment, and has a remarkably high level of self-esteem. He is after all the head of the nation, extremely wealthy, and successful in his political manoeuvres. He may even consider himself to possess high spiritual qualities; but gold has a double meaning in this regard: it can imply spiritual value, but it can also suggest materialism – an over-dependence on the material wealth of the earth.

Breast of silver: The heart, traditionally considered the seat of the emotions. The king's own opinion of himself on an emotional basis, though high, does not match his intellectual convictions. He may have feelings of guilt, knowing he has hardened his heart against the pleas, in particular, of the neighbouring tribes he has oppressed. They would certainly say that he was hard-hearted.

Belly and thighs of brass: The seat of instincts and base passions. Even in his own estimation he is somewhat brazen by habit, in his appetite both for food and for sex. Brass was considered a war-like metal – the metal of the war-god Nergal (Mars). With his brazen belly and thighs he is wont to trample on or even swallow up those who displease him.

Legs of iron: He goes where he will, without consulting the wishes of others. He is well aware that he tramples over the rights of defenceless people, especially those who have been conquered in war, and this again is a cause for guilt.

Feet of clay: After two and a half thousand years, this has come to mean that someone in a position of privilege has proved unworthy: they have shown that they are 'only human'. When in his dream the rock of materiality struck the image on the feet – the stone that turned into a mountain that filled the earth – the weight of materiality was set to deal him a shattering blow. It could be said of Nebuchadnezzar that he was caught up in the political momentum initiated by his father, and it was proving too much for him. Daniel might have concluded that the king was heading for a mental breakdown, and indeed, as far as we can tell from the records, this is what actually happened.

Nebuchadnezzar's dream of the great tree *(Daniel, 4)*

THE KEY TO DREAM ANALYSIS

Some years later Nebuchadnezzar had another *Great dream*, and again he found it very worrying. In the morning he sent for Daniel, and this time he narrated the dream himself:

Thus were the visions of mine head in my bed: I saw, and behold a tree in the midst of the earth, and the height thereof was great. The tree grew, and was strong, and the height thereof reached unto heaven, and the sight thereof to the end of all the earth: the leaves thereof were fair, and the fruit thereof much, and in it was meat for all: the beasts of the field had shadow under it, and the fowls of the heaven dwelt in the boughs thereof, and all flesh was fed of it. I saw in my visions of my head upon my bed, and behold, a watcher and an holy one came down from heaven; he cried aloud, and said thus, Hew down the tree, and cut off his branches, shake off his leaves, and scatter his fruit: let the beasts get away from under it, and the fowls from his branches: Nevertheless leave the stump of his roots in the earth, even with a band of iron and brass, in the tender grass of the field; and let it be wet with the dew of heaven, and let his portion be with the beasts in the grass of the earth: Let his heart be changed from man's, and let a beast's heart be given unto him; and let seven times pass over him. This matter is by decree of the watchers, and the demand by the word of the holy ones: to the intent that the living may know that the most High ruleth in the kingdom of men, and giveth to whomsoever he will, and setteth up over it the basest of men.

Daniel's interpretation was quite straight forward. He presented it as a warning to the king against an excess of pride and arrogance:

The tree that thou sawest which grew, and was strong....: It is thou, O king, that art grown and become strong: This is the interpretation, O king, and this is the decree of the most High, which is come upon my lord the king: That they shall drive thee from men, and thy dwelling shall be with the beasts of the field, and they shall make thee to eat grass as oxen, and they shall wet thee with the dew of heaven, and seven times shall pass over thee, till thou know that the most High ruleth in the kingdom of men, and giveth it to whomsoever he will. And whereas they commanded to leave the stump of the tree roots; thy kingdom shall be sure unto thee, after that thou shalt have known that the heavens do rule.

Despite so vivid a warning, it must be all too easy for any man in so powerful a position to brush aside any possible intervention of fate or higher powers, and think "I did it my way!" But it took a whole year for the impact of the dream and its memory to fade. Nebuchadnezzar, again full of self-adulation, found himself reflecting on his achievements, his power and majesty, when the prophecy struck home:

The same hour was the thing fulfilled upon Nebuchadnezzar: and he was driven from men, and did eat grass as oxen, and his body was wet with the dew of heaven, till his hairs were grown like eagle's feathers, and his nails like birds' claws.

Some commentators have claimed that the dream suggests that the king was suffering from lycanthropy – a form of madness that causes sufferers to behave like an animal (not necessarily a wolf) – and it certainly seemed to be predicting a spell of mental instability, or breakdown. In the event, it is likely that his courtiers would have looked after him during this period of madness. He was certainly highly thought of as a ruler, having restored the power of Babylon very effectively during his reign. Some have understood the prediction 'let seven times pass over him' as referring not to seven years, but to seven lifetimes – seven consecutive reincarnations to be spent as an actual beast; but the Book of Daniel records that the king was restored to sanity and to his kingdom after the appointed times, and continued to rule until his death in 562BC. There is a diagram of this dream in the section on *Dream diagrams*.

BIRDS

In all times and places where superstition has played a large part in daily life, birds have habitually been thought of as omens, and some traces of these ominous allusions can be recognized even in civilized lands today: magpies may be thought to predict several different kinds of fate dependent on the number that gather together; owls are said to be harbingers of death, and ravens too are supposed to foretell death, danger or disaster; storks are supposed to bring good luck, and newborn babies. The 'ominous' connection with birds relates to the fact that, being free to fly around, they are liable to appear almost anywhere at any time, and this makes them ideal as harbingers of whatever possible message we may have in mind.

To people everywhere, no matter how sophisticated they may seem, particular birds tend to call to mind specific associations, some based on ancient tradition, as the white dove of peace and relief from trouble. We may recall the story of Noah who, when the flood was abating, first released a raven which flew away never to return; then he released a dove which found a green sprig of olive and flew back to the ark with it. Referring to *Biblical dreams* we will remember the baker's dream in which a flock of birds predicted his death by devouring the loaves he was taking to Pharaoh. Wild geese irresistibly bring to mind far away wild and marshy places; the 'blue bird' has come to signify happiness if it flies around a house or perches on the roof; the *Parrot* is in a class of its own, as are the *Eagle* and the *Cockerel*. If you have definite ideas about birds of different kinds, if they remind you of some or other human function, or if they always seem to behave in a certain way, in your dream they may represent that function or type of behaviour for you. Different nationalities have different bird symbols of this nature. Birds, it seems, can vary from cruel and rapacious (think of vultures – or perhaps great flocks of small seed-eating birds that sometimes devastate a peasant farmer's crops), to gentle and lovable; their voices range from the delightful songs of one to the harsh croak or screech of another. A large white bird flying away is a universally held symbol of the human soul leaving the body. Dead birds almost equally universally signify lost freedom, lost hopes – a situation such as marriage which has become routine and restrictive. But most live birds as dream symbols, like omens, can mean whatever the individual unconsciously assumes them to mean.

See also: ANIMALS

BLOOD   *Essence and energy*

The vitality and driving passions of life may be symbolised by blood, and in some systems of religious thought or spiritual understanding a person is considered to possess different 'bloods' representing different basic passions: these symbolic bloods are not all red – red is merely the colour of the energetic, aggressive and defensive passion. The passion of learning and observing, or its blood, is thought to be white; the life-blood of sexual passion is considered to be yellow; the life-blood of greed and material possession is said to be black. If dream-blood seems to have changed colour, its message may follow these lines. Typically, though, dream-blood is the real physical blood that keeps us alive. A person bleeding or wearing blood-stained clothing in a dream usually signifies the onset of illness connected with the heart. Clothes of a faded or dull red can imply that the wearer or onlooker in the dream has been worrying about their health, but the potential illness is not presenting an immediate danger.

See also: DOCTOR

BOAT *The means of riding over water*

Water as a dream symbol represents the feelings – emotions and sexual impulses. A boat symbolises a person's passage over these sometimes troubled waters.

If you dream your boat is floating smoothly over deep water

The very fact that you have dreamed about it implies that you are feeling some apprehension; it suggests that you are well aware of the depth of emotion or passion beneath you, and feel the need for caution.

If you dream of a large ocean liner

In days gone by, these large ships became established as the obvious symbol of overseas travel, and so, by implication, an indication of a complete change of life scene, a thorough uprooting of everything familiar. Now of course, their place has been taken by jet airliners, and large sea-going ships are typical of leisurely holidays – and thence of a welcome change of scene, but not a permanent change.

THE KEY TO DREAM ANALYSIS

If you dream of sailing over stormy waters

This suggests that you are currently passing through a very stormy phase in your emotional relationships. You seem to have become very deeply embroiled in some scene which you may find difficult to back out of. Your feelings are being 'tossed around'.

If your boat capsizes in the dream

The implication is that some emotional or sexual situation in which you are involved is proving 'all too much', and you are being swamped by your own feelings, your own turbulent passions. In any event, as with all 'dream-boats', the symbol will probably prove to have a very personal meaning.

BOG   *A very sticky patch*

If you dream that you can see a bog

(Or a quagmire, a slough, a morass, a marsh, or a mire – the dream symbol may be given a variety of names), take it as a warning that there may be sticky times ahead. A situation exists in real life which must be avoided for your own safety or security. The dream symbol calls for a change at least of emphasis, if not of direction, in your everyday life. Mud itself symbolises an excess of emotional or sexual impulses which are saturating the ground, and affecting your environment. A bog has the added element of plant life on the surface which in a dream implies the struggle for existence and the feelings of arrogance or aggression that often go with it.

If you dream you are standing on quaking ground

Solid ground represents the solidity of materiality; on a personal scale it represents the security of your normal situation in life, your job, your marriage, your relationships, your living conditions. There may have been a *Trigger event* recently to make you doubt the reliability of things you used to depend upon. This could be classified as a *Warning dream*.

THE KEY TO DREAM ANALYSIS

If you dream you are plunging ever deeper into mud

The implication could scarcely be clearer: you need to consider a change of direction regarding whatever you most closely associate with these muddy conditions. The symbol implies that your actions or behaviour have in some respects become unpleasant, even to yourself. If this is the case, a reappraisal of your lifestyle is overdue!

See also: MUD

BONES   *The basic framework*

As a dream symbol, bones can have several very different connotations: they can imply the 'bones of an idea' – something new that is being planned; or they can imply the discarded remains of something old and no longer of use. They can also represent the strength within a scheme, the firm basis upon which an enterprise is founded. The *Theme mood* of your dream may help to explain the personal meaning of your dream symbol: if you recall the feeling of regret, or wistfulness, bones may represent the hopes and ideas you once had, but which came to nothing – something which you remember fondly and would perhaps like to resurrect. Dreams of bones can also involve a play on words – we speak of something being 'near the bone', meaning that it is rather hurtful, or we may 'have a bone to pick' with someone when we have a dispute. A bone featuring in your dream may also be a special sort of bone made known to you in the dream, and this will provide a clue.

See also: SKELETON

BOOKS   *Feeding the mind by reading*

Dream books almost always signify their own contents – the facts, the stories and ideas inside them – and a shelf full of books may represent a person who is full of ideas, a 'storehouse of knowledge'. In *Spiritual dreams* you may perhaps dream of being given a book which will show you whatever answer you need, in words or pictures. In more mundane dreams a book will represent an important piece of knowledge you may be searching for, the information you urgently need. In a few cases, a background of books may symbolize a comfortable situation of some kind, or a privileged lifestyle carrying the implication of material wealth – but a background of knowledge and a wealth of ideas is the more usual interpretation. There are exceptions which will be entirely personal. Quite commonly, if you pursue some particular subject or interest and like to read about it, a display of books in your dream may symbolise an extension of your opportunities in that direction.

See also: LIBRARY

BREAD *The staff of life*

In countries where bread is not the usual staple, other food commodities such as rice or maize may take its place as a dream symbol. Its meaning is likely to be 'the basic means of living', and of course the term 'bread' can also mean 'money'.

If you dream you are well stocked with bread

This reflects your own feelings about your current life situation. It may be a *Predictive dream* telling of an imminent upturn in your fortunes – though it could equally well have the nature of a *Wish fulfilment dream*, when it could prove to be no more than an expression of hope.

If you dream you have run out of bread

The implication is that your usual means of earning a living has disappeared, or is liable shortly so to do; your supply of 'bread' is drying up. This symbol is most likely to reflect your worries about security, or your own current fear that your position in life is not altogether reliable.

If you dream that your bread has gone stale, or mildewed

This dream reflects, or predicts, a disappointing situation; the remuneration or reward you had been expecting does not seem to be materializing. Perhaps someone on whom you have relied to supply an income or a regular service has let you down, or will shortly do so. In this case you need to start looking for a new source of 'bread'.

See also: FEAST; FOOD

BRIDGE   *The means to surmount an obstacle*

If you dream of a bridge over water

Water symbolises emotions and sexual desires, and a bridge across usually means that you are feeling anxious about some emotional encounter in your life. It implies that you do not really want to enter the water and get too wet: you do not want to become too involved. It may well refer to a sexual hang-up which you find troublesome, some issue that you would rather not face directly. The water in the dream may provide a clue. Dark or muddy water implies guilt and a sense of wrongdoing. Clear sparkling water shows that feelings of guilt are not involved, but you would still rather avoid what you see as a tricky situation.

If you are looking down from a bridge

Take careful note of what you are looking down at; what you are crossing over. Whatever it is will probably be the crux of your dream. The dream bridge forms a very useful function, enabling you to take a clear look at whatever is bothering your waking mind, whatever you are anxious to avoid. You might be looking down on a busy main road, and the implication may be that you do not wish to follow the crowd. Perhaps you have been feeling superior to the popular view about some issue, or feel that you wish to be alone to pursue your own interests in peace. Or you might be looking down on a quiet country lane or a lonely track, and this could carry the opposite meaning: you have been feeling somewhat isolated and would prefer to join the crowd and play a more active part in mainstream society. A railroad track running beneath the bridge can imply that you feel the need for a complete change of lifestyle: you need to get away from your current situation! If you are looking down at water running beneath the bridge, refer to the previous paragraph. The dream episode seems to imply that you have been feeling very emotional and rather apprehensive about the future.

If you dream you are beneath or looking up at a bridge

Bridges often feature in dreams when your waking life encounters difficulties. A *Fugitive*, or someone who feels in some way an outcast of society will dream of a bridge which, if attained, can provide a means of overcoming social isolation and rejoining the world at a more rewarding level. A bridge overhead always reflects a feeling that there must be a better way forward, particularly if the ground beneath is unpleasant to walk or drive on, perhaps muddy or flooded with unpleasant emotions. Try to remember if the dream bridge featured anything that might offer further clues.

See also: FORD; ROAD; STEPPING STONES; WATER

BROOM   *A means of removing dirt*

Dirt, clutter, unwanted characteristics, unwanted people – a dream broom can represent a helping hand or a circumstance which seems about to remove any of these things. As the dreamer, you may be looking at the broom or the sweeper as though you yourself are part of the clutter to be swept away; or you may be the one doing the sweeping. The distinction will be obvious to you in the dream. The old saying 'a new broom sweeps clean' often applies when somebody like a new employer, or a newly appointed manager, wishes to reduce the workforce and is looking very keenly at standards of work and relationships. The dream can reflect the anxiety felt by those in line for redundancy.

See also: DIRT

BUGS *Parasitic insects*

In America it is usual to call all insects 'bugs', but strictly this term should be reserved for those insects with sucking mouthparts. Whether these are plant-bugs or human bed-bugs, they are parasitic creatures in the sense that they suck the life-blood out of whatever it is they are feeding on. To dream that horrible insects are feeding on your own body, or are infesting your bed and personal belongings, seems to imply that you are aware that something – it may be an unwanted person or an unexpected circumstance – is taking advantage of you and using you in a way that you deeply resent. Similarly with a plant-bug; you may have a cherished plant, and find that these creatures are drawing out the sap which keeps the plant healthy. The plant in your dream may symbolise your own family, your business, or you yourself, and the implications are the same – you feel that some unwanted presence is taking advantage of you and sapping your resources. By itself, the dream offers no solution to the problem, but merely reflects your concern.

See also: ADVERSARY; ASSAILANT; INSECTS

BULL *A powerful masculine animal*

Unless you are a cattle farmer or a bull-fighter in real life, in which case the dream may be merely setting the scene for you as a normal everyday situation, a bull usually symbolises a man whom the dreamer is nervous of offending. In the normal way, such a 'bull-man' may be no trouble at all, but he could well prove dangerous if annoyed or challenged – not necessarily in a physical sense; it may well be a matter of business. If in your dream you find yourself tiptoeing or walking warily around a seemingly docile bull, this is likely to be the connotation: the symbol is reflecting your present concerns rather than warning of trouble ahead. A bull charging along and looking for trouble is a different matter – this could well be a *Warning dream* implying that an angry character – or a male with powerful passions – is liable to cause you problems.

See also: ANIMALS

THE KEY TO DREAM ANALYSIS

BULLYING   *Intimidating another person*

If you are the bully in your dream

The implication is that you have been acting in some unfair way, causing another person unnecessary anxiety or suffering. Perhaps it is only their feelings that are being hurt, but one's own *Inner feelings* take this situation very seriously, as it causes unbalance in your own *Self*. careful thought is needed to identify the problem. It may, however, be a *Balancing dream* in which the dreamer is compensating for feelings of helplessness in real life.

If you are being bullied in your dream

It may simply mean that your peace of mind is often upset, and you disapprove of the way other people behave. But if you are actually suffering from bullying in real life the dream may be pointing out a possible course of action. Now is the time to decide to do something positive about it.

If you recognize the dream-bully as a real person known to you

There may be no real bullying as far as you are aware, either by this person or his associates, but it seems your own *Inner feelings* are being disturbed by his actions, or by your own relationship with him (or her). The dream offers you a chance to take a calmly objective look at the situation.

See also: *Adlerian dreams;* ADVERSARY; ASSAILANT

BULRUSHES   *Plant cover at the water's edge*

Water symbolises the feelings; pond or streamside vegetation symbolises a place, or an attitude of mind, in which to hide from powerful feelings. From this hiding place, whatever is affecting you can be observed or felt, but you are hoping to remain uninvolved personally. Bulrushes or reeds in a dream usually seem to be hiding something – perhaps some wild creature representing your own sexual passions. Certainly something with a strongly emotional content is liable to emerge from it. Moses was supposed to have been found as a baby hidden among the bulrushes, and he went on to found a culture that has grown to embrace the Jewish, the Christian, and the Muslim world, while in stories of mythology other heroic figures of achievement have been given a similar origin. Typically, rush-like plants feature in a dream when something highly significant seems about to emerge from a strongly emotional situation.

See also: WATER

BURGLAR *An unwelcome intruder*

It is not unusual for a burglar to feature in a dream, and as a simple expression of anxiety the implications of intrusion or loss of privacy or possessions are fairly obvious.

If you dream that an unknown burglar is getting in

This may reflect your own worries about security, and the building where the burglary seems to be taking place may be your own home, or that of someone else closely connected with or reliant upon you. This is a straightforward, practical dream advising you to improve security. But it may also represent worries that your secrets are in danger of disclosure, and that you have been feeling guilty about something you would not like to become public knowledge.

If you dream that the burglar is known to you

The implication is that the person concerned seems to be interfering in your private affairs. It may be that bureaucracy or the law is involved in this. Any dream which features real characters known to you needs personal interpretation by thinking round all the details very carefully. The burglar breaking in may be yourself in disguise; you may be projecting your fears or feelings of guilt onto someone else; you may even be meddling in someone else's affairs – and only you can know the truth of the matter.

THE KEY TO DREAM ANALYSIS

If you are prowling around in someone else's property

The chances are this dream reflects some recent situation know to you. Have you been trying to find out details about some organization, or perhaps an acquaintance? The implication is that you are not too sure of your ground. You may not have feelings of guilt, but you do feel deep down that you are in the wrong. Perhaps the dream is hinting that you need to be more open about your intentions.

See also: ASSAILANT; ENEMY

BURIAL   *Disposing of the evidence*

If an official ceremony is involved

To dream of a burial is always unlikely to predict an actual death. The most likely implication seems to be that some important episode of your life is coming to a close, and that a new set of circumstances with new opportunities are about to arise. An important ceremony involving lots of people reflects the fact that the closing episode does indeed involve others. Take note of these people's reactions and attitudes, and your own feelings, as these will provide important pointers.

If the burial is a very simple affair

Unless there are other indications, the dream seems to be implying that you are pushing something out of sight – something that might be better made public. Other people may be involved in the dream burial, but the grave could still be representing your own *Personal unconscious mind*, in which perhaps you are trying to bury matters that should have been dealt with during waking hours. Matters which are suppressed by your conscious mind may become 'repressed' and cause psychological problems later on. The dream is warning you to take careful stock of your own attitudes.

See also: CORPSE; DEATH; FUNERAL; PIT

C

CACTUS   *Any thorny or prickly plant*

Cacti and other prickly succulent plants tend to grow in desert-like places with very dry conditions, and if you study the *World dream* and *Adlerian dreams* you will see that plants growing in these conditions can carry a very powerful hint of the internal power struggle. You may be feeling rather like a cactus plant yourself, forced to survive in unrewarding circumstances and defending yourself against the assaults of others, real or imaginary. This dream may be telling you to have more confidence in yourself and in your friends and colleagues, and look for a practical way out from your problems. There is probably no need to be so defensive. But any thorny or prickly plants featuring in a dream symbolise dangers and difficulties which may be very real in your daily life. By itself the dream symbol is offering no solution, but simply reflecting your own feelings.

See also: DESERT; FOREST; SAND

CALENDAR   *A record or diary of days and dates*

There is always a hint of urgency in this symbol. It is reminding you of the passage of time for a reason. It can be a reminder that your time is limited and there are still many things to do. It may be reminding you of an important date or anniversary that you are in danger of overlooking. There are sure to be other factors in your dream which offer a clue. Calendars and diaries can refer backward as well as forward, and the symbol may be pointing out the significance of some past event that has suddenly become relevant in your life. It may be a reflection of the general feeling that 'time is running out', that a chance has arrived to lift your situation in life to a new level, perhaps with spiritual connotations. Two calendars together carry a powerful message of two people meeting, paths crossing, and fates intermingling. Keep days, dates and times in mind when interpreting a dream of this nature.

See also: CLOCK; CROSSROADS

CANDLE

If the three chief symbols of religion could be said to be faith, hope and love, a lighted candle represents hope, a reflection of the heart and its emotions.

If you see a lighted candle

This symbol is rather akin to the symbol of a light at the end of a tunnel: it expresses a glimmering of hope and expectation of better times to come. The imagery of a distant candle in a window guiding travellers lost in the dark is powerful, however unrealistic it may be.

If you are lighting a candle in your dream

Sentiment is burning in your heart, and your emotions are reaching out towards some person or perhaps a worthy cause. In days of old, lighting a candle was a simple means of seeing in the dark, and though nowadays largely obsolete, as a dream image it can still imply inspiration or revelation, perhaps a new understanding. 'A candle in the wind' can be taken to mean one person's efforts when struggling against overwhelming odds, and this may be your own sentiment regarding your current position in life. On the other hand, a whole bank of candles, or candles floating on the water such as may be seen at some religious ceremonies, imply that you are not alone in your expression of hope, and that communal emotions are running very deeply.

See also: ALTAR; CARVINGS; STATUE

CAR   *A personal means of travel*

If a car is your own normal means of travel

For many people the automobile is an essential means of getting about, and driving everywhere has become second nature to them, almost like an extension to their legs. This makes their car a very useful dream symbol, because anything that happens to the car, or obstructs its progress, or makes driving in the dream difficult, reflects what is happening to them in real life. It represents the progress of your own self through life, and very clearly expresses your hang-ups, your day-to-day problems, your indecisions and certainties. If you run off the road, have an accident, break down, or run out of fuel, any of these will very clearly relate to your own behaviour, your health, and general fortune. Your car may be humming along on a smooth clear road, or churning through the deep mud, avoiding potholes or edging its way over rocks. Sometimes you may find the road running out altogether, and you will know that your lifestyle is running into serious difficulties; a change of course will be essential for your own well-being.

If you have a passenger in your car

There may be real people known to you riding in your car – family perhaps, or friends – and in this case the dream is pointing out that their lives have been affected by you, making you to some extent responsible for them. However your passenger may be a somewhat obscure figure, and not someone known to you in waking life. If you are taking a policeman in your car, the dream is telling you that your present course of action is morally correct, but at the same time warning you that if you are tempted to cheat your own conscience in some way, you will not escape the consequences. Complete strangers featuring as passengers in a dream may be *Archetypes of the unconscious mind*, parts of your own psyche representing your higher, intuitive self. In this case it is important to heed their advice if they have any to offer, and the dream needs interpreting very thoughtfully. If your dream passenger turns out to be someone frightening and undesirable, pay careful attention to this, too. It will be a part of your own psyche making its presence known.

If you are riding in someone else's car

If the driver is a real person already known to you, the implication is that you have become in some way dependent upon them in waking life. If the driver is completely unknown to you, it would be as well to take careful note of this person's characteristics. He or she may be an unfamiliar part of yourself, perhaps the *Persona*, which is dictating your progress through life at the expense of your real needs. It may be that you are trying to conceal some aspect of your own personality.

If you do not normally drive a car

Cars normally travel on roads, and these highways represent the main thoroughfares of life – the direction the vast majority of people are heading. If you feel yourself in some way at odds with this mainstream flow of life in the dream, the symbol is probably very accurately reflecting your own attitude to others. This is in itself is neither good nor bad. If you are struggling to make progress, constantly impeded by other people's cars, perhaps you need to make an effort to fit in with the rest of the population. You may, however, be humming along very well without a car of your own, even outpacing everyone else, and the dream is drawing attention to the fact that you are not so materially orientated as the majority. Try not to lose touch with hard reality!

See also: ACCIDENT; DRIVING; FLYING; JOURNEY; MUD; ROAD;

CARNIVAL *A fantastic procession*

If you are taking part in the carnival

Carnival is a tradition which allows people to forget their problems, let their hair down and have a good time without too much responsibility. It represents a time when fantasy and sheer imagination is allowed to take precedence over boring day-to-day affairs, and moral restrictions are allowed to slip. The dream could be hinting that you have been ignoring your responsibilities and being a little selfish by putting your own pleasures first. But carnivals may appear to be more easy-going than they actually are; they need a great deal of preparation and dedicated energy, so are not really conducive to relaxation. You may be thinking of adopting a change of routine in real life that seems an easy option, but in practice it could well prove to be tough going.

If you are a bystander as a carnival goes past

Are you, the dreamer, looking disapprovingly as others enjoy themselves? Or perhaps you would like to join them if only you could? Whichever it is, the dream is reflecting the fact that you have been feeling left out of things in your waking life. It may be that you need to take a more lenient view of other people's behaviour, to relax a little and not take a strictly moralistic view all the time.

See also: MARKET; PROCESSIONS

CARVINGS *Artefacts resembling a person or thing*

The *Collective unconscious* often makes use of dream symbols depicting carvings or figurines, often made of wood or ivory. They tend to represent something the dreamer would rather not identify or think about directly. They may carry the idea of ancient wisdom, or possibly superstitious beliefs that belong to the past. In effect they are symbols *of* symbols that have been taken too literally in the past, and should now be seen for what they are. Quite often a dream carving can be understood as a phallic symbol referring to some sexual situation that the dreamer feels guilty about. They may have broader implications too, particularly if the carving is of some recognizable person, creature or thing. It may carry the implication of feeling restricted, of being obliged to accept a mere representation of something or someone the dreamer would love to know at firsthand. In ancient times carvings were thought misleading, or even wicked, because it was believed that naive people might worship them. This idea, long hidden in the *Collective unconscious*, is at the root of the carving as a dream symbol. It represents something made by human hand that might take on an independent life, or an ability to influence, all of its own. Try to remember all the details of the dream carving to see if it will offer clues.

See also: IDOL; STATUE

CATHEDRAL *A large and imposing church*

As a dream symbol, its meaning will largely depend upon the dreamer's own past experiences, and what the idea or sight of a cathedral brings to his or her mind during everyday life. There may be some particular association which springs to mind, and this of course will have a strong bearing upon the implications of the dream. Unlike churches, cathedrals tend to symbolise authority and establishment, the laws of morality and ritual. They are not as a rule cosy places where the ordinary church-goer can feel at home. They carry with them the air of special occasion and hierarchy, but are also very powerful symbols of devotion and a sense of awe. Following a dream involving a cathedral, careful note should be taken of the emotions which accompanied it, and they will provide a clue. As with most other dream symbols, if you have known a person who was closely associated with a particular cathedral in the past, this person could well have a bearing on the interpretation of your dream.

See also: ABBEY; ALTAR; CHURCH

CAVE   *A natural space or opening inside rock*

A cave can symbolise different things for different people, but it always refers in general to a hidden, secret place of concealment. In waking life, a cave is hampering and restrictive, and not really suitable for a long-term stay. To find yourself inside a dream cave is to be enclosed or trapped within solid materiality, a place in the dark where the future is uncertain. As a symbol it could apply to your social situation, to your career, your health. It could be a temporary hiding place away from society, and imply that the dreamer is experiencing a period of depression.

If the cave seems a welcoming place

The dreamer may feel under threat in some way, and wishing to escape and be hidden from view. To a male dreamer, as a place of refuge a cave can symbolise his own mother – a place of safety where he could retreat as a child, but indicating the need in adulthood to break away from her dominating influence and claim true independence. Take careful note of the emotions associated with the dream cave, for these may provide a clue.

If the cave seems a threatening place

Some unknown danger may lurk in the cave – perhaps even a distant folk memory of the Stone Age family seeking refuge and remaining watchful lest a cave bear should be inside: this is one possibility, carrying the implication of a *Reincarnation dream*. Far more likely, though, the cave represents the dreamer's own *Personal unconscious mind*, and the danger lurking inside is the dreamer's *Personal shadow*. In this case the unknown horrors in the cave are already part of the dreamer's own psyche, and really need to become known, when they will no longer be a threat.

See also: ABYSS; ADVERSARY; CELLAR; DUNGEON; PIT; TUNNEL

CELLAR   *A basement or underground room*

In dreams, the *Self* is often seen as a house. The normal living quarters of this house represent those conscious parts of your mind which you normally experience, your everyday thoughts and feelings. The upstairs rooms or perhaps an attic represent the higher possibilities of your own psyche. The cellar which you rarely or never visit represents the unconscious part of your mind. If you consider the concept of *Yin and yang*, the cellar is the yin, the dark, mysterious feminine place which receives and reformulates the impressions of the conscious, male yang.

If you become aware of the cellar but do not enter it

This dream image implies that you would prefer not to meet the dark side of yourself: you feel the need to present yourself in the best possible light, and feel the need to keep certain aspects of your character hidden. You may have problems which you do not wish to face directly – problems which you should deal with before they become a burden to you.

If you enter the cellar in your dream

To analyse this symbol you need to remember all the details of your time in the dream cellar. What did you do there and what did you see? Or if it was too dark to see, what did you fear or suspect might be hiding there? The *Personal shadow* lives in your dream cellar, composed of all the things about yourself that you have refused to accept as your own. If this dream figure were to emerge, he or she could prove quite horrifying, but it needs studying and thinking round very carefully if good is to come of it.

See also: ABYSS; CAVE; *Cycle of the dreaming self;* DUNGEON; PIT

CHASING   *Pursuing or being pursued*

If you are chasing someone in your dream

The dream symbol is fairly explicit: you are trying to capture something, achieve something which is eluding you. The question is: what? There will probably be other powerful clues in the dream which will help you identify the thing you are after, and possibly also tell you how best to go about securing it in real life.

If you are being chased in your dream

This is a surprisingly common dream experience, because most of us normally try to avoid some confrontation or another, and symbolically run away from it. A dream symbol such as this is related to the symbol of the *Assailant*, with perhaps a hint of the *Adversary*. It may relate to some recent waking experience when you overstepped the mark in some way, and fear facing the consequences. If it is something deeper, hidden in the *Personal unconscious*, you may not even want to identify it or find out its true nature – but if it continues to disturb your sleep, you really need to clear the matter up so that it can be expelled from your mind. The only sure way to find out the true nature of this dream pursuer is to allow it to catch you. After experiencing a dream of this sort, think round the characters and features of the dream very carefully. You may find you can 'ask yourself' for another dream of this nature so that you can allow the pursuer to catch you, and then see what happens. However, as this will give rise to a *Lucid dream*, take care you do not influence the outcome with your ordinary ego. Allow the dream to run its course if you can.

See also: ESCAPING; FUGITIVE

CHILD *A very young person older than a baby*

As with so many other dream symbols, the child in your dream may represent a real child, perhaps a family member or one with whom you come in contact. But in cryptic dreams the innocent child or a *Baby* may be an *Archetype of the unconscious mind* – an aspect of your *Personal unconscious mind* – yourself as you would be, if free from outside influences. The dream symbol of a young child may also represent something, some attribute or new idea, that has come to your awareness. You can be sure that a dream of this nature will be very important to you, psychologically and spiritually, and you need to analyse it very thoroughly.

Children's dreams

In early childhood, remembered dreams are of great interest because they sometimes reflect the *Myth-making dreams* of mankind throughout the ages. Young children obviously lack experience of the world; but if you were able to measure the 'level of spirituality' of people, you would certainly find that children possess a much 'higher' level than most adults. To put it in religious or perhaps sentimental terms, they are 'closer to God' than the rest of us and are thus able to receive dreams which are not influenced too strongly by materiality, by the sophisticated influences all around us. Dreams recounted by young children tend to sound like sheer fantasy to adult ears and are usually dismissed as no more than that; but as often as not the dreams of young children recall the *World dream*, and their own spiritual descent from the original pristine high-human status (the mythical Garden of Eden) into the world of nature, and through progressively more worldly stages. *"I was a boy but I ate some monkey food and then I was a monkey"* or *"I went for a ride on a tall giraffe and it carried me into the jungle".* These are not the sort of things that most dream-workers wish to hear about – the intricacies of evolving relationships and developing psychological traits seem to be absent. Such dreams, however, are far more telling than the longest, most convoluted adult dream of everyday relationships. But inevitably children go through the usual learning process and gain experience of the world, and all too soon the adult perception of dreams as a learning, or potentially liberating process comes to apply equally to young people. The early myth-making dreams of descent through the world of nature will normally have run their course by the time the child has reached the age of seven or eight. Increasingly after this their dreams will feature real places, and exploits with their friends. Children too can be markedly intuitive, a faculty which shows itself in dreams, usually involving family relationships, when they may share something of their parents' experiences – past, present or even future – featuring in their own dream world. Young children can of course be very suggestible, and anything said or done to a sleeping child, particularly during a period of *Rapid eye movement*, is likely to feature or intrude in their dream. The results are liable to prove vivid enough to be remembered into adulthood. In strict moderation this suggestibility can be used in a constructive way, perhaps warning of some danger to which the child is particularly susceptible. A parent might repeat such a warning in a quiet, authoritative voice, using a short, easily memorable and unequivocal phrase such as "Remember fire!" if the child is fond of playing with matches, or "Beware the road!" and this will have a positive effect. But the message needs to be positive and reasonably specific. One should *never* issue general commands such as "Do as you're told!" in these circumstances, because it could have a most unfortunate effect on the developing child's self confidence and sense of judgment. Any kind of hypnotic command could have far-reaching and very dangerous results, and should be strictly avoided.

See also: Family dreams; Family intuitive dreams;

THE KEY TO DREAM ANALYSIS

CHURCH *A modest place of worship*

If the church is in use and flourishing

Your own normal understanding of a church and its functions will have a strong influence on the nature of the church as a dream symbol. At two extremes, some people look on 'church' with something approaching contempt; others think of it as something noble, a place of high aspiration. When attempting to interpret your dream involving a church, you will base your conclusions on this type of preconception. At best, the dream church will carry a message of enhanced spiritual understanding and the path of submission to a higher will than your own. To dream of entering a beautiful church and feeling at peace implies just this. Unpleasant or disturbing dreams of church call for some honest self-appraisal. Other things related to church, such as towers, spires, singing choirs or pealing bells, can all carry much the same message as the body of a church itself.

If the dream church is ruined and abandoned

An ivy-covered ruin may seem romantic, but it carries with it powerful images of emotional certainties long gone. As a dream symbol a ruined church building tends to suggest an obsolete set of beliefs, or perhaps the feeling that spiritual revival has passed beyond recall. The dream may hark back to childhood, and may even represent a parent on whom you can no longer depend when in trouble. Your feelings may be sad and nostalgic, but the dream itself will probably indicate a new level of understanding, a new set of certainties coming to reality, not necessarily about religious matters. Very often the church symbol refers to human relationships which have become somewhat over-emotional.

See also: ABBEY; ALTAR; CATHEDRAL

CLIMBING *Trying to achieve a higher position*

The track that you follow in your dream represents your own path through life, and if you are travelling along a steep section of that path, it can only mean that you are experiencing a difficult or frustrating period in real life. It may be of your own choosing, an attempt perhaps to reach a higher position in career or society.

If you dream you are in difficulties on your climb

You may seem to have been in danger of falling or having reached a point in your climb where you could not go on. This is a warning symbol relating to your life: your own aspirations are leading you astray in some respect. It sometimes happens that one 'bites off more than one can chew', or is trying to achieve too much at work and feels in danger of falling out of favour. You will probably know whether you seem to have taken a wrong turn in real life, and your everyday situation needs careful re-examination.

If you are climbing a mountain in your dream

As a rule, no-one *makes* you climb a mountain. It is a voluntary effort, and the same principle applies to climbing a dream mountain. The great majority of dreams involving climbing reflect the dreamer's waking efforts to attain a better position, a better situation in life, the achievement of some ambition. It might relate to everyday life when this seems to involve heavy going: marriages sometimes seem like this, when you are making a big effort to accommodate someone else's feelings and needs. Gaining the top of a hill implies that things will soon get easier on the downhill slope. Ice and snow on the top reflect the fact that you seem to be experiencing an unrewarding phase of life, but circumstances are liable to change soon and for the better. A mountain very obviously can symbolise a difficulty to be overcome in practical terms.

If you feel you are ascending a holy place

The symbol of climbing can also have a more spiritual meaning: the mountain may be purely abstract, and the act of climbing it will have significance only to the inner dimension, the soul. This is where the positive symbol of a mountain as a difficulty to be resolved becomes a negative one: if you are voluntarily climbing a mountain in your dream and you believe this to be a 'spiritual' symbol rather than a material one, you are probably climbing the wrong mountain! If you seem to be in danger of falling or sliding back down in your dream, take this as a gentle hint that you are tackling the subject in the wrong way. A 'spiritual mountain' simply cannot be climbed by effort of will, because desires of this sort belong to the material or occult and not the spiritual world. Your own experiences, hopes and fears in everyday life should make the meaning of your dream clear, and if this analysis still seems nonsensical to you, ask yourself for another dream that will make the matter plain. The entry on *Incubating dreams* may help.

See also: LADDER; MOUNTAIN; OBSTACLES

CLOCK *A timepiece*

A very telling symbol, which almost always relates to something very important in the dreamer's life. Time is a basic concept, an indication and a warning pointing to opportunities, consequences, *Trigger events*, and fate itself. As a *Mandala* it can represent the dreamer's whole life, material, physical, psychological, and spiritual. There comes a time in anyone's life when the fateful hour strikes, and all the dream details should be recalled and pondered over. It is important! (It could represent something that seems normal and everyday, like a time or date that should be remembered – an anniversary perhaps – and the dream is telling you that trouble lies ahead if you neglect to take the appropriate action). The substance of the dream clock may be significant: whether it is a rich antique, jewelled or made of gold, or perhaps plain and ordinary, or even rather cheap and nasty – these will be pointers to the 'quality of the moment' and the nature of the trigger that has prompted the dream.

If there are two clocks together in your dream

It is likely that one of those clocks represents yourself, the other symbolising some other person who is currently featuring strongly in your life. Two lines of fate have run together and could be pointing towards a single destiny. The meeting point is the trigger for a new start in life, a completely new direction.

See also: CALENDAR; MANDALA

THE KEY TO DREAM ANALYSIS

CLOTHES *Outward appearances displayed*

If your own clothes are in question

Our own clothes represent the way we present ourselves to the world, our *Persona*, our own private disguise, our social facade, the way we think of ourselves and the way we think others may sum us up. It is quite common for people to dream that they are searching through their belongings to try to find the right clothes to wear, and finding nothing really suitable. A dream such as this implies that you are finding it difficult to fit in to the social scene, or whatever situation you find yourself in. Taking on new responsibilities for instance, facing up to problems, finding a new job perhaps: these are occasions when the dreamer may search in vain for the right clothes to wear. The symbol means you are lacking in confidence, worrying about whether or not you will fit in to the new situation, or what other people will think of you. Others tend to see you as you present yourself – your face value – and the way in which you project yourself is really up to you alone. We can only be really happy if we accept ourselves as we really are, but, society being what it is, we cannot always expect others to see it that way. Our dream clothes may also reflect our fears, sorrows and anxieties: a widow may dream of a black wedding dress; someone worried about illness may dream of discoloured or red clothes. It is a very personal symbol.

If you dream of other people's clothes

Like an actor's costume, clothes in a dream sum up the nature or character of the person wearing them. They represent the qualities and passions which you believe that person to possess. Important people, or higher *Archetypes of the unconscious mind* in your dream may wear very impressive robes to stress the fact that what they have to offer may be of great value for your waking life. If the dream characters are real people known to you, their clothes will represent the way in which you think of them. If they are obviously imaginary or obscure dream characters, their clothes will symbolise the qualities or situations they are fulfilling in the dream.

See also: FASHIONS; HAT; NAKED

CLOUDS

Fog or mist seen in a dream show that the future, the physical or practical way ahead, is obscured and cannot yet be known by the dreamer. Clouds however, being normally above one's head, refer to a different dimension: they refer to an unknown situation that exists or may exist above the dreamer's knowledge, a higher status in psychological or even spiritual terms. If someone you know seems in a dream to have climbed or risen through clouds, the implication is that this person has somehow attained a higher state that must remain unknown to the dreamer. Similarly, light billowing clouds seen in a dream express ideas that seem light and fantastic but may prove important in unforeseen ways. Dark storm clouds, perhaps with flickering lightning on the horizon, have often been reported by dreamers who were shortly to experience troubled times, a fairly obvious premonition which may feature in a *Predictive dream*, or a *Dream of the future*.

See also: FOG; MIST

COCKEREL   *A crowing rooster*

For thousands of years people have kept domestic poultry, and the crowing of a cock or rooster has become firmly entrenched as a symbol of new dawning – a wake-up call. It can also be a symbol of arrogance, or 'cockiness', of 'blowing one's own trumpet', the proverbial cock on the dunghill, lording it over his hens. It can also symbolise empty boasts, or even betrayal, as in the Christian story of Peter's thrice-denial of Jesus before cockcrow. In all cases the symbol represents a proclamation, an announcement of something that may be either good or bad. Your dream should tell you which in your own case: at best it may be the dawning of new possibilities, or at worst merely an empty boast on the dunghill of life.

See also: BIRDS

THE KEY TO DREAM ANALYSIS

Collective intelligence

When you take up dream analysis, and try seriously to interpret dreams for others, in all probability you will soon become aware of this amazing human capacity. It is connected with the idea of the *Collective unconscious*: at a certain level of the psyche, a great deal may be shared in common. The famous John Donne was hinting at this when he wrote 'no man is an island, entire of itself'. It is not a belief, or a theory, it is an experience, and it is most likely to come to our awareness when we concern ourselves with the dream world. For instance, it might be that you have been reading about the dream-work of Freud, or Adler, or Jung, or some other lesser known dream-worker, and learnt about the symbols and themes and methods most familiar to them. Then if someone presents you with their dream for analysis, you will find that it corresponds with the specialist material which you happen to have read about, and with which you are now familiar. In other words, that person will have dreamed a dream not for themselves but for *you* to interpret. Similarly, their dream may contain information that is plainly intended for *you* rather than for them. Things like this can happen because all humanity, at the deep level of the *Inner feelings*, is itself linked in a way quite unsuspected by the everyday waking mind. This is the sort of information that can only be confirmed by personal experience.

Collective unconscious mind

Sigmund Freud formulated the theory of the unconscious mind as a part of the psyche that retains material forgotten or disowned by the conscious, aware mind. Carl Gustav Jung took the matter much further by separating the ideas of the *Personal unconscious mind* from the collective unconscious. The personal unconscious mind is just that – it contains material pertaining to the individual person. The collective unconscious mind contains material of a similar nature but common to the whole of humanity. It is from this vast sea of unconscious material that the *Archetypes of the unconscious mind* may emerge. For our everyday dreams of relationships and personal behaviour, the *Inner feelings* draw the images and scenes familiar in our dreams from the personal unconscious; but when we are fortunate enough to experience a *Great dream,* far more vivid and meaningful than ordinary relationship dreams, the inner feelings will have selected the images and symbols from the collective unconscious itself.

Compensatory dreams

These types of dreams are in some ways related to *Wish-fulfilment dreams* in that they tend to express the dreamer's hopes and longings, and they resemble *Adlerian dreams* in that they express the dreamer's wish to experience qualities they do not normally possess. It sometimes happens that a person who leads a quiet, sheltered life may experience dreams of a violent and adventurous nature; or the opposite – a hyperactive person may dream of peace and tranquillity. A gentle person may dream of inflicting violence; a chaste person may dream of sexual indulgence. A dream of this nature is unlikely to contain much in the way of useful information, beyond simple psychological release.

See also: Balancing dreams

Concern (A theme mood)

One of the major theme moods of what are probably the most commonly experienced types of dream. Concern dreams express exactly that: concern over some situation, some state of affairs that is not going exactly to plan, or a period of doubts about the future that the dreamer is going through. It may well relate to another person close to the dreamer emotionally, when there are some worries about that person. Such a dream may act as a trigger for the dreamer to take appropriate action to improve the situation. But a concern dream will probably not in itself offer any solution to whatever may be troubling the dreamer, though when a dream is vivid enough for the emotion to be remembered, the mood of the dream may change towards the end – concern giving way to relief or hope, or joy, when some plain solution to the problem seems to be emerging.

Conscientious dreams

The inner self is the seat of conscience, and your own *Inner feelings* – which some would call the 'higher emotional centre' of the psyche – are the source of dream images, the normally unconscious part of yourself that is able to select symbols, incidents and themes which link together all your everyday experiences and are projected within your own awareness as dreams. Anything you do during the day which is not really fair, anything worthy of blame, anything carrying guilty feelings which you did not want to face up to during waking hours, all these may well be pushed away by the conscious mind and disowned – but they do not disappear, they filter instead into the receptacle of the *Personal unconscious mind* where they are sifted and sorted by the hidden inner feelings, eventually to be re-presented as dreams. Any dream carrying an unpleasant feeling of guilt or remorse will fit into this category.

Contempt   (A theme mood)

Whether in a dream or in waking life, this is a highly unpleasant emotion, whether felt about people or situations. If the feeling persists after waking, the dream needs thinking through very carefully. It may be advising you to be more broad minded in your dealings with others. Even if it seems well justified, the person who shows contempt is behaving in a contemptible way because he or she is feeling 'holier than thou'. Sometimes in a dream the attitude of contempt is being directed towards the dreamer – also a warning to see matters from the others' point of view.

Controlling dreams

The principle of 'control' implies using the conscious will, the ego, to bring something about, and when studying, recording and analysing your dreams in the hope of gaining something of real value from the lessons you learn, 'control' is the one thing that should be avoided. If you work at it, certainly you can learn to control your dreams, to create *Lucid dreams*, to give your own ego and self confidence a boost, to overrule your *Inner feelings*. To do this is to short-circuit the dreaming process. The inner voice is very readily shouted down, and lessons to be learnt from studying the unconscious cycling process at work within your own psyche are very easy to ignore. In this day and age great importance is given to the ability to control, to take power, to make the decisions. But in studying dreams and your own dream-life, submission is the key: submission to the highest part of your own self, which is *not* your everyday intellect. If there is a valuable lesson to be learnt, why throw that chance away by further boosting your own sense of importance?

CORPSE *Death*

If the corpse is of an unknown person

If no obvious meaning springs to mind, take note of whether the surroundings of the corpse in the dream were familiar to you, or if they represented an everyday situation for you. If so, the dream implies that something which you had, some abstract quality or line of business perhaps, is no longer available to you. If the surroundings are completely unfamiliar, the dream may be informing you that someone known to you is suffering a similar sense of loss. It may even have happened that you were dreaming of another person's experiences. There are of course all sorts of circumstances by which you may be experiencing or fearing death on a day-to-day basis, and the meaning then will probably be only too plain.

If the corpse is of someone known to you

You may dream that someone close to you lies dead, and this may reflect your fears and worries. It may be that you are being over-protective about this person. The implication may also be that the feelings of affection between you are effectively dead, and this will be a wholly personal matter. Very religious people may have this dream when they fear that the person concerned does not share their feelings of faith.

Also see: BURIAL; DEATH; FUNERAL

COW *Domestic cattle*

The cow is a powerfully significant symbol in many world cultures. It may reflect the *World dream* by symbolising the animal life forces as they relate to human beings. In Pharaoh's dream (see *Biblical dreams*) it represented fertility and the agricultural cycle. To a farmer, it may set the scene of a dream as reflecting an everyday situation. The symbol of a cow is liable to emerge from the *Collective unconscious* as a representative of motherhood in the sense of a sustaining Mother Earth – the fertility goddess who appears in many guises. It can represent pregnancy, or the wish to become pregnant. It can also represent gentle femininity, and is unlikely to refer to a woman in any derogatory sense. It should never be confused with the symbol of a *Bull*, which carries a very different meaning.

See also: ANIMALS

CROCODILE   *A monstrous beast*

A frightening creature from the swamp – a crocodile, alligator, giant lizard, even a dinosaur – when it appears in your dream should seldom be taken at its face value. The chances are it will represent a part of yourself, coming to awareness perhaps from the *Personal unconscious mind*, or the *Shadow*. It will probably represent some characteristic, some set of emotions, that you had thought were long gone and forgotten; something perhaps that you would not wish to acknowledge as part of your own nature. You might dream that you look over a familiar wall, or perhaps into your own garden, and find it full of nameless horrors. Dark desires that you try to suppress are liable to lurk within the recesses of your unconscious mind, and build themselves up into this frightening form. If they really do represent an innate part of yourself, the only way to deal with such a dream creature is to identify it and try to tame it in as harmless a manner as possible.

See also: DRAGON; MONSTER

CROSSROADS *A choice of directions*

A fork in the road carries much the same implication, suggesting a moment of choice, a crucial stage when we are forced to make a major decision about the way our own life is going. A crossroads can also represent a meeting-point when two or more people or principles meet up together, a point at which they can react, join forces, or go their separate ways. There may be an element of doubt or hidden danger about the crossroads too, some 'dirty work at the crossroads'. Ideas of this nature are liable to appear as dream symbols when they reflect your current situation. When you are in doubt about which road to take, a helpful figure may well appear in your dream to point out the best route. When this happens, you should take careful note of the outcome, for it will probably be one of the *Archetypes of the unconscious mind*, a *Wise person* perhaps, who can give you excellent advice if you are able to understand it.

See also: JUNCTION

CRYSTALS

Whatever crystals mean to you, this is probably the implication they will carry in your dream. Many people believe that crystals have special qualities of healing or even spiritual powers, and of course diamonds or other precious stones are also crystals. They certainly have value, but their value to our inner selves is a wholly material rather than a spiritual one. Your bodily health of course is largely a material matter, but it is easy to be misled by anything as attractive and interesting as semi-precious stones. If you feel very much attached to crystals in your dream, the message may be that you are putting your faith in the wrong direction, and ought to find out about your soul life – to look above material attachments and the values of this earth whilst still enjoying them.

See also: EARTH; JEWELS

THE KEY TO DREAM ANALYSIS

CUP   *A container to drink from*

The drinking utensil that features in your dream is a very basic symbol common to the whole human race. It draws attention to something that has entered or is about to enter the dreamer's waking life, some new understanding, some unforeseen twist of fate. Often, it represents an unpleasant duty or task that must be undertaken. The nature of the cup itself will give a hint as to the type of fate that is to befall. It may have a low and unpleasant nature, or it may equally be something of great and lasting value. It may perhaps have a misleading appearance of beauty whilst containing something rather unpleasant to drink. There are many different shades of meaning which the cup may be taken to represent, and its meaning as a dream symbol will depend entirely on the dreamer's own experiences and expectations, and of course on any other incidents which feature in the dream.

See also: VASE; WATER

Cycle of creation in dreams

This is connected with the concept of the *World dream*. Every individual during dreams is experiencing a personal cycle involving the conscious and the unconscious minds. We could say that the world itself is also experiencing a continual cycle involving the creation and development of the planet, the earth, the plants, the animals and the humans, and every individual potentially possesses the nature of this same cycle in miniature. Most dreams, those involving everyday affairs and relationships, could be said to be purely material dreams, equating to the basic geological structure of the earth. Dreams which show an inclination to rise above the mundane and involve something of a struggle for inner power and expansion, a growing away from the basic ground common to all, could be said to equate to the growth of plant life on the earth and the fact that plants are programmed to struggle against their competitors and claim their own place in the sun. Dreams which seem to be orientated towards a broader and fresher outlook, including perhaps a new concept of morality, with fantastic imaginings and intellectual efforts, could be said to equate to the animal life of the earth, with its free-ranging mobility. Dreams which contain images from the *Collective unconscious* and seem concerned with a yet broader perspective, or an overview of the world, could be said to equate with the life of human beings on earth. The next stage, dreams of the *Human world of spirit*, represent the culmination of the dreaming process as a means of advancement. So, looked at in this way, the great majority of our dreams can be seen to be of a material nature, dreams in which the cycle of creation is not functioning on an individual basis. If we pay attention to our dreams, record them and try to understand them, we can show willing to help this great cycle sweep us along with it, and include us in its process of psychic development. The more conscious our dream life, the more our psychic selves will be in tune with the cycle of creation.

Cycle of the dreaming self

Sigmund Freud and Carl Gustav Jung laid the foundations of this concept and made it much easier for us all to understand how the dreaming process works. Imagine yourself as a circle or a sphere, a globe like the earth, with the upper sunny side bathed in light. This bright upper half represents your ordinary waking self during the day, full of thoughts and emotions – your conscious mind. The lower half of your personal globe will be in darkness, and this represents your sleeping self, and your unconscious mind. Everything that has come to your attention during the day, and especially matters that worried you or seemed to you important, or things that you tried to ignore or avoid, all these matters, or the memory of them, sink down into the dark recesses of the unconscious mind where they are studied by the hidden *Inner feelings*. Here they are worked upon, compared, evaluated and categorised, put into a fresh context, and in that new form fed back into the conscious mind by way of dreams and insights. The inner feelings are also known as the 'higher emotional centre' and this term probably gives a better idea of their great importance in affairs of the psyche. But even they cannot always cope. Matters that cannot be dealt with, perhaps memories that are too dark and unpleasant to be accepted by the emotions, tend to sink down to the very bottom of this *Personal unconscious mind* where they become part of what Jung called the *Personal shadow* – the unpleasant hidden part of yourself that you do not want to accept as part of yourself at all. This hidden part of the personality is the source of nightmares, of demons and monsters and frightening opponents that may seem to threaten you during your dreams. This personal cycle of the dreaming self continues non-stop throughout the day and night, but it is when the conscious mind is sleeping that the solutions to any problems you may have experienced during the day can be resolved. Dreams progress during the sleeping period while the inner feelings do their work, and jumbled thoughts and emotions become arranged in an understandable form. *Evening dreams* seldom make sense. *Dawn dreams* on the other hand are rich in meaning and value as they usually draw on psychic material from outside the self.

See also: Spherical symbols of the self

D

DAM *A great volume of water held back*

Water symbolises the emotions, the feelings, also the sexual desires. As a dream symbol the dam indicates that very powerful feelings are being held back and controlled – possibly by strength of will-power, by determination not to let your feelings show, perhaps by social or moral restrictions. There is plainly some good reason in waking life why these particular feelings should not be allowed to run free, but the situation could be a dangerous one. If the dam should burst, if you can hold back no longer, an uncontrollable flood of feelings will be released. This is the nature of dams: what should by nature be a steady trickle or smooth flow of water, is transformed into something potentially very powerful, something which could prove unstoppable. The dreamer will probably know what the dream is referring to. Perhaps a way can be found to release some of the water to avoid possible disaster.

See also: WATER

DANCE

There are basically two types of dance: those which stem from the *Inner feelings*, and those which arise from the passions. You could say that the one is spontaneous while the other is contrived. To dance from the inner feelings in your dream is showing you that your dreaming self is not controlled by materiality, or by the desires.

If you are dancing alone in your dream

The everyday type of dancing in your dream will depend largely on your own experience and expectations of dancing in waking life. To dance on your own may indicate that you are keeping something secret from others, and warning you not to be too aloof. Perhaps you have been less than sincere with the people you normally mix with.

If you dream of dancing with others

To dance with another person in your dream usually indicates sexual desire for them which cannot be expressed in any other way. You may, of course, be a regular dancing partner and the dream is merely setting the scene with a situation that is familiar to you. Communal dancing, line dancing, square dancing, these may have a more subtle meaning in your dream. If the dancers form a square or circle this could be a *Mandala* of your own self, and you need to study all the dream factors very thoughtfully.

See also: BALLET; THEATRE

DARKNESS

One normally sleeps in conditions of darkness, but when darkness features as a dream symbol it can prove rather frightening, with a sense of being lost, bewildered, and helpless. It implies that your way forward through life is being hampered and you cannot see what should be done. But, like night itself, darkness tends to be relieved after a while, and the dream may be telling you to have patience as the situation will soon improve. A particularly nightmarish dream of darkness, particularly when you cannot equate it to any real-life situation, can refer to the unknown part of your own self, the *Personal unconscious mind*, and the darkest part of your own psyche, the *Personal shadow*. This is waiting to be explored by you in your dreams, and the experience may prove of great value to your long-term psychological well-being. You certainly need to take careful stock of your current situation. A *Dawn dream* involving something frightening that seems to be emerging from the darkness always needs careful consideration.

See also: ECLIPSE; LOST; TUNNEL

DARTS   *Aiming at a target*

Assuming you are not a great darts player in real life (in which case a game of darts may set the dream-scene as a normal everyday experience), the dream symbol of throwing darts has a very clear meaning: you are aiming for a certain target which you may hit or miss in the dream. Your dream darts and dartboard may be referring to some specific aim, or they may be symbolising your efforts in life to achieve normal standards of living, expectations, social, moral or financial.

See also: DICE; PLAYING

Dawn dreams

If you study the *Cycle of the dreaming self* and the *Development of dreams* you will realise that the formation of dreams is a cyclic process – that is, it progresses and gathers momentum throughout the sleeping period as the thoughts and feelings and sensations of the day are assimilated and worked over by the *Inner feelings*. The longer this process lasts, the more vivid and constructive one's dreams can be expected to be. The inner feelings normally draw on the contents of the *Personal unconscious mind* to produce dream symbols reflecting everyday events and experiences that can be re-presented to your conscious mind with a new twist on their meaning. For more vivid and meaningful dreams this 'higher emotional centre' is able to draw on images from the vastly more extensive *Collective unconscious,* and dreams of this nature are most likely to be dawn dreams. Arriving just before you awake in the morning, they are particularly intended to be remembered by your everyday mind: a dawn dream is warning you to sit up and listen! They will very likely be telling you that a chance has arrived to improve yourself, psychologically or spiritually. *Reincarnation dreams* and *Non-self dreams* are also likely to be dawn dreams, imparting information that may be utterly unfamiliar because it will have arisen by way of unknown factors outside of the self. An attitude of submission in the face of the unknown is essential for such dreams to be understood. Don't dismiss them as figments of the imagination: value them! Personal experience of *Great dreams* which arrive at dawn should ensure that your dream-life will never again be dismissed as irrelevant.

DEATH

Death of a non-human

Powerful hopes and fears can trigger dreams, and the death in your dream may be a product of your everyday outward emotions being expressed in this way, rather in the manner of a *Wish-fulfilment dream*, but with negative implications. But a dream arising from the *Inner feelings* which portrays the death of some creature may be a reflection of the great *World dream*. A child may dream that an animal has died, and this will illustrate the fact that he or she is growing up, and approaching the age of puberty.

Death of a human

In dreams the symbol of death may not refer to the death of the physical body. It is more likely to imply the "death" of some particular phase in your life, and points to new beginnings. It can also imply that some human faculty is no longer functioning as it should, and the other details of the dream need to be recalled and analysed carefully.

See also: BURIAL; CORPSE; DARKNESS; FUNERAL

DEMON *A terrifying apparition in your dream*

Do demons exist in fact? They certainly do in dreams, where a demon constitutes an *Archetype of the unconscious mind,* and is one of the many forms which the *Personal shadow* can take when it makes its presence known. It is made up of all the factors – thoughts, feelings, fears, faults and failings – which have been rejected or denied by the conscious mind. These factors do not exactly 'come back to haunt us' because they are already within our own psyche and have been there all the time, steadily consolidating and strengthening their nature beneath the surface of awareness until sooner or later they emerge in this frightening form. Any process of 'atonement', psychological or spiritual, aims to tame and assimilate this symbolic figure.

See also: ADVERSARY; *Terror;* WITCH

THE KEY TO DREAM ANALYSIS

DESERT   *A barren inhospitable place*

The dream symbol of travelling through a barren place tends to reflect your own thoughts and feelings about your current life situation. Perhaps you feel powerless and undervalued, at a loss to know what can be done to better your position, and you feel your patience giving way to bouts of irritation and anger. The dream symbol itself is not hinting at what can be done to improve your lot, and you need to pay careful heed to any other features in the dream. If none of this applies to you, however, and your dream desert is insistent, it can only mean that your inner life is lacking some sort of spiritual contact. You need to seek to rectify this in waking life, and recording and paying heed to your dream-life is a move in the right direction.

See also: *Adlerian dreams;* SAND

Despair   *(A theme mood)*

A feeling that 'things are getting on top of you', a sense of hopelessness; if this is the theme of your dream, the prevailing mood, you will of course interpret all the features and events of the dream in that light. If there are no recognizable features other than this feeling of despair and emptiness, and you are giving vent to these feelings in the dream, it could be acting as a catharsis for your emotions which have been building themselves up – a release of pent-up emotions. But if you are merely experiencing these emotions without actually expressing them, the dream could be advising you to be more open about releasing your emotions during your waking life. Sorrows which are expressed freely are not so damaging to your psyche as suffering them in silence.

Development of dreams

Once you are aware of the *Cycle of the dreaming self*, and when you learn about the mysterious *World dream* behind it all, you will have no difficulty appreciating the way in which the dreaming process develops through the night. From the initial chaos of the dozing-type

Evening dreams, those dreams which start to take shape during the early part of the sleeping period will reflect the nature of materiality – they will tend to be about things and places and normal everyday occurrences. Dreams occurring later will show something of the 'plant' nature, that is, they will express aggression and the constant struggle of competition. Later still dreams may also display competitiveness, but being of an 'animal' nature they will be more concerned about socializing or communication with others rather than aggression, and they may have a moral flavour. Towards dawn dreams will reflect a more constructive quality. They may not be pleasant for the dreamer, but they are most likely at this time to present solutions to any problems he or she may be experiencing in waking life.

DICE

As a symbol of taking a gamble and resting in the hands of fate, rolling dice could scarcely be more explicit. As a dream symbol, it will probably relate to some circumstance with which the dreamer will be well aware . The numbers that come up may have their own significance, and again they will relate to the dreamer's own experience. We are all to some extent being swept along by the current of fate, and the hoped-for outcome may not be forthcoming. If you throw the double six in your dream this may be a *Wish fulfilment dream*. If you have been fervently hoping for some particular outcome in real life, your own conscious ego may have intervened and tried to swing the dream hoping to influence events; it is unlikely to be a *Predictive dream* of the future.

See also: PLAYING

DIGGING *Penetrating the ground*

You may of course be a gardener or trench-digger in real life and the dream symbol is setting the scene as one with which you are familiar. More likely, though, it will relate to knowledge, some secret perhaps which you wish either to hide or to uncover. The ground represents solid materiality, thoughts and memories.

THE KEY TO DREAM ANALYSIS

If you are doing the digging

The symbol is probably referring to some mystery that has fascinated and baffled you in waking life. You may have forgotten something you thought vital and have been trying to remember it. In effect, you are trying to penetrate your own *Personal unconscious mind*. Try to remember your feelings during the dream: were they feelings of hope, or anxiety? Were you trying to locate and uncover something of great value, or perhaps some guilty secret that has been worrying you? Perhaps you are searching for your own past, your roots? Only you can answer these questions.

If someone else is doing the digging

Again, your own feelings during the dream will give you a clue. If you are merely a spectator at the dig you are unlikely to be interested in somebody else's search for their own secrets. More likely, you believe that they are trying to uncover your secrets. Assuming you have not really buried a body in the back yard, you have perhaps been worrying lest people find out about something you would rather remained private. Is there a skeleton in your closet?

See also: ARCHAEOLOGY; BONES; BURIAL; PIT

DIRT

It is natural for your *Personal unconscious mind* to contain something akin to dirt, and your *Personal shadow* in particular is made up of factors, feelings and ideas which you thought unworthy or disgusting and did not like to acknowledge as your own. A particularly moral person may feel that anything which does not conform to his or her ideas of morality is in some way dirty. The dirt which you dream about is more likely to have an abstract nature than to be real tangible dirt, and the other incidents in your dream should point to its nature. Dream dirt may be localized: you may have dabbled in something of which you are ashamed, and you will dream that your hands are dirty; you may feel aloof over other people whom you believe to be less competent than yourself, or perhaps you are convinced that you have got rid of some fault or other that bothered you in the past, but which in fact is still influencing you In cases like this you may suddenly notice that your feet are dirty and clearly visible to others. Those other people may have noticed the dirt and this may be embarrassing you in your dream. Take it as a gentle warning to avoid criticising others!

See also: *Disgusting dreams;* EXCREMENT

Disaster dreams

Something akin to a *Nightmare*, everything will seem to be going wrong in a disaster dream; disaster itself is almost the emotional theme forming a background to your dream. If there are recognizable events, look at each of these separately and try to identify the problem in each case; if there is a common theme, a common cause, this will be the important factor. If the dream events do not make sense at all, and seem mere excuses for the sense of disaster to continue, take it as a hint that you are under stress, and you need to adopt a more relaxed view of life, a more submissive attitude, an acceptance that 'what will be, will be'. It is of little use to worry over things you cannot control. So-called anxiety neurosis is at the root of most disaster dreams.

Disgusting dreams

All the features in your dream should be recalled if possible, and thought round carefully. They should give you a clue as to the source of whatever you found disgusting. You will know then whether the unpleasant situation is a 'one-off' or a regular ongoing circumstance; an aspect of yourself, or someone else in particular. A toilet situation that has become disgusting in some way is a common dream theme, and usually refers to some feature in your own personality which you do not like and would be better off without. You will be familiar with the *Cycle of the dreaming self,* and the *Personal shadow,* and realize in what way the disgusting dream element is related to your own subtle contents. Your dream life is working towards your own betterment, and is less likely to be concerned with someone else's psychic problems or moral shortcomings, though family problems may play a part by way of intuition.

See also: DIRT; EXCREMENT

Disorientated dreams

If the dream itself is chaotic

Sometimes your mind may feel in a whirl for whatever reason, and this feeling may transfer itself to your dream life temporarily. But in the normal way dreams tend to develop and become more orientated during the sleeping period (*Development of dreams*), and *Evening dreams* or dozing dreams, being still undeveloped, normally tend to be chaotic and meaningless to the waking mind.

If you feel disorientated in the dream

It is quite common to feel that you have lost direction, whether physically, socially, morally, or career-wise, and this feeling may well feature in your dreams. Your *Inner feelings* may be better equipped to deal with your sense of aimlessness than your waking mind, and your dream may be showing you what can be done about it. Recall and think round every detail of the dream, particularly if it was vivid and you experienced it towards dawn. If, however, you are suffering from a state of anxiety and disorientation in your waking life, you really need to calm yourself before going to bed, and allow your inner feelings to take command. Try to remember that everything is in the hands of a mich higher authority than our mere hearts and minds.

See also: LOST

Distrust   *(A theme mood)*

Suspicion can be a useful sentiment, warning us of possible dangers, and the feeling of distrust that seems to have permeated your dream may be doing just that – warning you to take care. Plainly, all the dream details need noting and thinking round very carefully. It may have happened that something which you have recently experienced, some situation which seemed normal and everyday at the time, may be misleading you in some way. Sometimes, however, the feeling of distrust in a dream may give way to *Relief* and acceptance, and this will be of great significance. You may have been worrying unnecessarily in real life.

DIVING *Plunging into water*

The dream symbol of *Water* refers to strong emotions and, it may be, sexual desires. Whether you are diving into water in the dream or whether you are merely watching others diving, the meaning is probably the same: 'taking the plunge' and committing yourself to these powerful passions. The dream itself should tell you whether the outcome will be good or bad, whether you should take the plunge or not. At this stage you cannot know what the outcome will be, but the practical wide-awake implications of the dream will probably be fairly obvious to you. Take special heed of any dream characters who appear. Are they real people known to you, or are you encountering an *Archetype of the unconscious mind*? Only you can decipher the full meaning of the dream and learn from it.

See also: WATER

DOCTOR

If the doctor in your dream is a real doctor known to you

The dream will probably be referring to a real medical problem which needs attention. Of course you may be very familiar with doctors and hospitals, and to dream about these would be an everyday dream for you. But for most people, if you have recently visited the doctor in real life, the dream may be telling you to think again about the diagnosis you received and the treatment you were prescribed: it may not be right for you and needs a rethink.

THE KEY TO DREAM ANALYSIS

If the dream doctor is completely unknown to you

This could be an *Archetype of the unconscious mind* conjured up by your *Inner feelings* and ready to give you good advice, but the advice is more likely to be about psychological or spiritual matters than physical problems. Spiritual well-being is something that the outer personality does not really know about, but it is very real, and if any advice is on offer, we need to take it very seriously. Nowadays morality is often pushed out of sight, but it is important to the inner self, and your dream doctor may be referring to this side of the psyche when he gives advice. Your own feelings on waking, the *Theme mood* of the dream, may give you a clue.

See also: BLOOD; HOSPITAL; WISE PERSON

DOG

Ancient symbol of the human-animal nature, dogs have been associating with people for thousands of years and fit in to our social systems very well. It is hardly surprising that they appear so regularly in our dreams. Referring to the *World dream* we can readily see that built into our own nature we have a certain affinity with the spiritual life-forces of the animal world. This affinity is likely to be portrayed by the dream symbol of the dog. In our dreams the *Personal shadow* can take the form of a dog, often, perhaps, resembling our own familiar household pet, only to make its demonic nature known after it has been petted and accepted: a reminder that our psychic contents, both good and bad, are not always what they seem. You may, of course, dream of a real, friendly dog, or perhaps a savage one, and the dream itself will probably make its own meaning plain.

See also: ANIMALS; DEMON; WOLF

DOLL   *A lifelike toy*

The dream symbol of a doll is a remarkably personal one, and most difficult to penetrate by anyone other than the dreamer. It probably represents you, the dreamer, but in an objective way, as though you are standing back and observing yourself unfeelingly. What is happening to the doll in your dream? Who else is involved? Is it *your* doll, or does it belong to someone else? You should ask yourself these questions when you awake. If there is a *Theme mood* during or immediately after the dream, this will provide a valuable clue as to the true nature of the symbol.

See also: STATUE; TOY

DOLPHINS

Creatures thoroughly at home in the sea: both dolphins and porpoises, probably seals and sea-lions too; we mostly think of them as playful and carefree, equally confident in rough seas or calm, supposedly intelligent and amazingly athletic. If they feature in a dream, they are probably referring to some group of people whom the dreamer admires, and whom he or she would rather like to join. But their social milieu is to us an unfamiliar one, and while they are indisputably masters of their environment they may not take kindly to intruders into their territory. They have an animal nature that can be cruel and uncaring as well as fun-loving. The dream could be a gentle warning to stick to the surroundings and company you know best.

See also: ANIMALS; WATER

DOOR

As a dream symbol, the difference between a door and an open entrance, or gateway, is that you cannot see through or beyond the solid door. You have no way of knowing exactly what lies on the other side. It may lead to a different level or state of being, a different lifestyle or cultural environment. The symbol of a door to be passed through often features in the dreams of those who have recently been bereaved, or in actual 'near-death' experiences. Sometimes there is the hint of something very pleasant on the other side. You may wish to go through the doorway but cannot, or perhaps you wake up before you can get through. Passing through an open doorway or a gate, on the other hand, usually refers to some new level of knowledge you wish to attain, and carries no hint of death. You know what is there and merely seek to attain it.

See also: GATEWAY

Doubt (A theme mood)

The feeling of uncertainty running through your dream, if it features a real-life recognizable situation, is reflecting the good advice to proceed with great caution. If the dream is plainly about a non-real situation, particularly if it features travelling or wishing to travel but being impeded, it implies that you have reached a *Crossroads* in your life, whether physical, mental, emotional, or spiritual. It sometimes happens that a feeling of doubt during the early part of a dream changes to a sense of relief or release, and the dream content needs recalling carefully, because there will be good advice hidden there waiting for you to find.

Dozing dreams

Especially when you are getting on in years and inclined to doze off in your chair, you may find that you are experiencing instant dreams of a somewhat chaotic nature. These are related to *Evening dreams*. They will seem to make perfect sense whilst you are experiencing them, but as soon as you wake it becomes plain that they are quite nonsensical. This is perfectly normal, and relates to the *Development of dreams* during the *Cycle of the dreaming self*. All the thoughts and impressions gained during your waking hours are still passing down into the *Personal unconscious mind*, and have not yet been sorted and characterized by the *Inner feelings* into a form which makes sense. Instantly forgotten, trying to recall them is like trying to grasp air, and even if you can, it will be of little use to try to analyse them.

DRAGON

The mythological dragon is a guardian of the *Personal unconscious mind*, however that concept might be expressed and described. Some cultures hold dragons, or their own national dragon, in great esteem, and the people of these cultures tend to keep their own subconscious contents well hidden and unacknowledged. Other cultures may have a mythological tradition of having killed a dragon which was holding them in thrall, and these people are usually quick to acknowledge their own hidden contents and aim to bring them out into the open. A clash of cultures may well result, because these myths are more than mere imagination on the part of our ancestors. So the significance of a dragon which features in a dream will depend entirely on the dreamer's own cultural background. The dream dragon is guarding a cave which probably holds a treasure, and this treasure amounts to the benefits that would ensue following the assimilation of one's own unconscious contents, resulting in *Psychic wholeness*.

See also: ABYSS; CAVE; CROCODILE; MONSTER; TREASURE;

Drawing dreams

It sometimes helps in recording and understanding a dream if you make a sketch of the dream scene as you remember it, soon after waking. If there are any details which may otherwise be forgotten or overlooked, it will ensure that they are placed where their true significance lies. if you are an artist, of course, you may be able to produce a full-colour tableau of events; but merely a simple pencil sketch will help. There might be several scenes as the dream changes. Try to avoid the tendency to make an 'itty-bitty' drawing in which the dream features are too widely scattered.

Robert dreamed that he was walking along a path at night between bushes and among sheep in a field. The light he was carrying went out when the plug jerked out of its socket and he stopped, but he could still see himself walking on, along a well-lit street. His drawing is shown on the opposite page.

THE KEY TO DREAM ANALYSIS

Dream diagrams

Most dreams, and especially the more complicated ones, prove easier to analyse and interpret when they are laid out in tabular form, or as a diagram with all the features linked. This process often brings out a meaning that would otherwise be overlooked. A tried and true method is to set out the dream incidents in order as they happened, or the dream symbols in the order of their appearance, linking those which seem directly related. Below and connected to these, set out the immediate impressions and obvious associations that spring to mind, and below these again set out the conclusions you draw from each. These linked sequences should lead to the overall message of the dream.

To take an example dream quoted in my book *Decoding your dreams*: Paul was an architect who had been worrying about problems with his heart and had a nagging fear that he might die before his latest ambitious project could be completed. This was his dream:

I was driving along in my car. The road was very potholed and muddy. I came to a crossroads and stopped, not sure which way to go. A railway line ran close to the road, and an empty train was standing there. *The old engine was wheezing and sounded as if it were breaking down. The engine driver got out of his cab and stood there uncertainly. He was an elderly man and wore a uniform of faded red. Then another man appeared at the side of the road, a stranger, well dressed and authoritative. He introduced himself, but I immediately forgot his name. I asked him the best way to go. He got in the car with me and pointed out the best road, and I drove on. Then we came to a town and I stopped. My passenger advised me to buy some flowers, and I bought a bunch of lilies. I asked him his name again, but again I forgot it, and I murmured to myself, "This man is filling my mind with forgetfulness." As we stood there, a funeral procession came by. Then, suddenly, the people taking part in the procession stopped, abandoned whatever they were carrying, and strolled away, chatting casually among themselves. I realized that this had been merely some sort of dress rehearsal and not a real funeral.*

The dream symbols described throughout this book form the basics of Paul's dream: *Driving his car,* symbolising his normal progress through life. *The bumpy, muddy road* indicating that Paul was currently going through a 'rough patch' caused by his health concerns. *The crossroads* expressing his feelings of doubt about the best way forward, about the attitude that might restore peace of mind. *The empty train,* which might have been packed with other people all heading for the same place – perhaps to sample Paul's completed building. *The old engine driver dressed in faded red,* symbolising uncertainty about his own health. *The confident stranger* who got in Paul's car and showed him which way to go: this enigmatic figure was the archetype of the wise man – Paul's own higher intuitive self whose name was to remain a mystery. His identity could not be made known because he belongs to Paul's unconscious mind. *The advice to buy flowers,* and by choosing lilies which have a symbolic association with death, Paul was facing up to his fears. The dream *funeral procession* which he was able to observe as a bystander, and which was abandoned by the people taking part, indicating that it was not yet to be made a reality. All these factors added up to a very important lesson for the dreamer, and yet in itself it was the type of dream that could easily have been forgotten, or rejected by the conscious mind as a mere jumble of unrelated images.

THE KEY TO DREAM ANALYSIS

Identify the separate incidents as they happened in the dream and set them out sequentially. Then from each one of these draw your own conclusions: *Driving:* your journey through life; *Crossroads:* decision time; different choices to be made; *Empty train:* the potential for many people to travel or experience something; *Wheezy old engine:* is this referring to your own physical health? And having plotted the whole dream in this way, draw further conclusions from the conclusions you have already drawn:

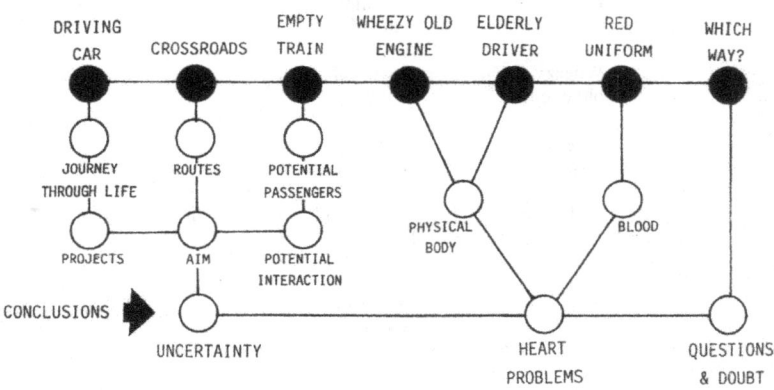

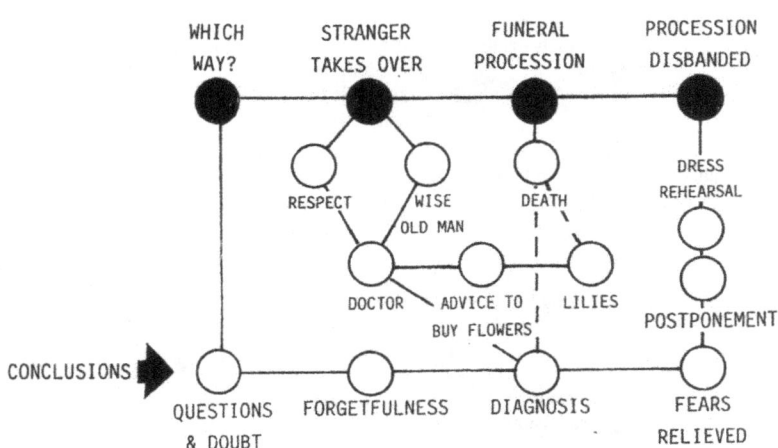

THE KEY TO DREAM ANALYSIS

Theme	Sequences	Conclusions	Emotions
	Driving a car	Paul's journey through life	
	Bumpy road	Going through a worrying time	
	Crossroads	Uncertainty	Anxiety
Concern	Empty train	Potential for public interaction	
	Wheezy old engine	Doubts about future	
	Elderly train driver	Lack of physical confidence	
	Red uniform	Threat of ill health	Doubt
	Wise man	Paul respects wisdom of his passenger	
	Indicates the best route	His own higher self can direct progress	
	Forgets name	A source of wisdom not available to the conscious mind	Puzzlement
Reassurance	Advice to buy flowers	By buying lilies Paul accepts the inevitability of death	Acceptance
	Filling his mind with forgetfulness	Exchanges anxiety for deference	
	Funeral procession	Paul's fears being faced	
	Funeral disbanded	His fears are unfounded	Relief

THE KEY TO DREAM ANALYSIS

Probably the best-known dream in the world is the *Biblical dream* that Pharaoh experienced and was famously interpreted by Joseph, as recounted in the Book of Genesis. After seven good years Egypt was to suffer a seven-year drought because of failed annual floods by the River Nile. Pharaoh himself was a living symbol of Egypt, and in this sense his dream predicted the fate of the whole country of Egypt rather than himself as an individual, and it was in this light that Joseph interpreted the dream. Pharaoh had dreamed of seven fat cows which came up from the river to graze in the lush fields. These were followed by seven thin cows which ate up the fat ones, and yet remained as thin as before. Check back to Pharaoh's dream of cows on page 46. Had Joseph produced a dream diagram, it might have looked as follows:

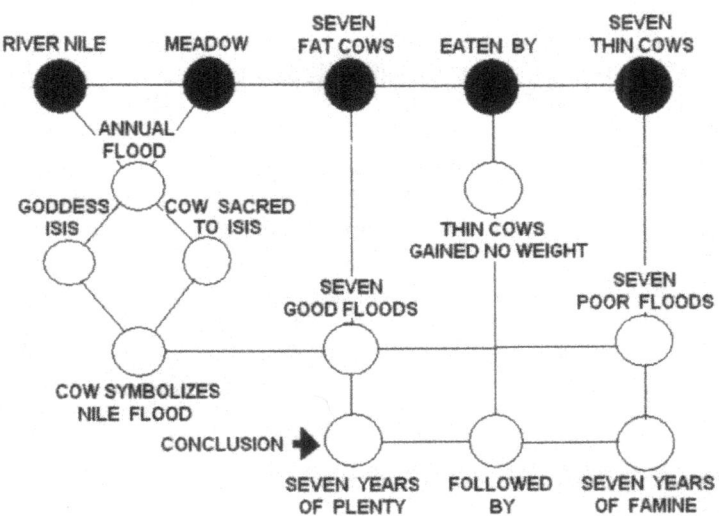

Another remarkable Biblical dream (in the Book of Daniel) which was complicated enough to need a diagram to help with its interpretation was the Babylonian king Nebuchadnezzar's dream of a great tree, interpreted to him by the captive Israelite wise-man Daniel. Again, as king, Nebuchadnezzar's dream reflected the fate of his country as well as himself. But in this case it seemed to portray his personal descent into a type of madness which did not result in the dissolution of his country. That was to come some time after his reign through military action (foretold this time by the waking vision of a moving finger writing on the wall while a feast was taking place). In Nebuchadnezzar's case, if the event really happened, his courtiers and ministers were able to keep the country running during their king's period of incapacity – reminiscent perhaps of England's king George III during the period of the Regency early in the 19th century. This is not recorded in the Old Testament account, but the Babylonians certainly thought highly enough of their King Nebuchadnezzar II to support him through his difficulties, as he had achieved a great deal for their city state, and ancient historians believe this to be the case.

The dream itself is related in detail in the section on *Biblical dreams*, and featured a great tree which fed and sheltered the living creatures of the area. A heavenly command came to chop down the tree, but to retain the stump, held secure by an iron band. The dream told how he would be obliged to live as a beast, unkempt and witless, until 'seven times had rolled over him', and until he had learnt that fate lay in higher hands than his own. Apparently he had to learn humility. There is a reflection here of the *World dream* by which a 'tree', or the plant kingdom, is seen to symbolise the characteristic of power-seeking in humans, bestowing aggression and arrogance through the strongly competitive nature characteristic of the natural instincts of plants.

If Daniel had drawn a diagram of the dream, its sequence and conclusion could have been as follows:

THE KEY TO DREAM ANALYSIS

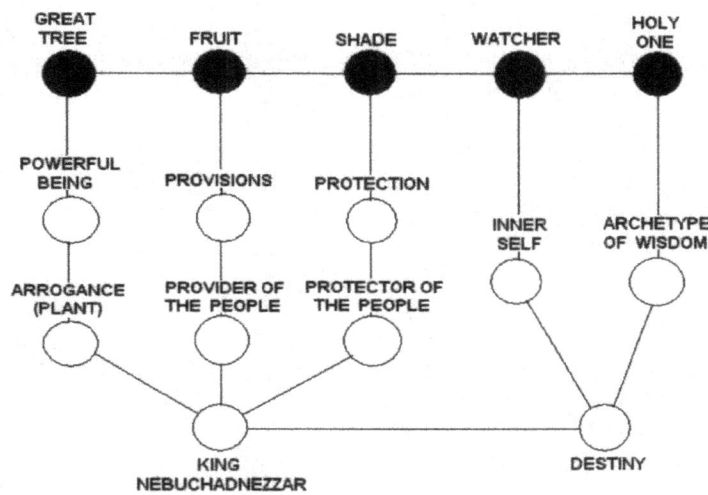

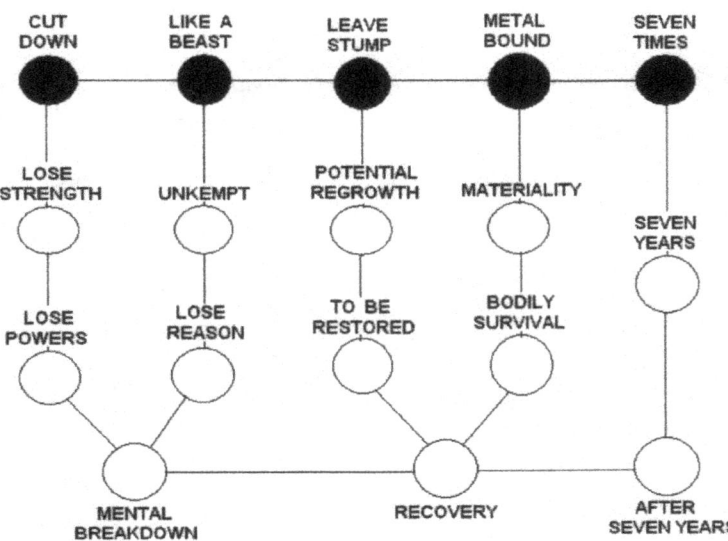

DRIVING   *Being carried by your vehicle*

Driving a car is second nature to very many people, and as a dream symbol it represents one's personal progress through life. The car itself symbolises the solid materiality of the human body, and the road symbolises the progress of life and the incidents encountered along the way. For people who do not drive, much the same meaning is to be found in taking a bus or a train, riding a bicycle or a horse, or merely walking along the path. The incidents met with along the way, the state of the road, the behaviour of other road users, these will all need a strictly personal interpretation, for only the dreamer will know about the real-life things that have happened and are happening to him or her. To dream of driving other people symbolises that the dreamer has or feels a certain responsibility towards them, particularly if they are members of the family or colleagues. Being driven by someone else implies the opposite: the dreamer is in some way reliant upon the person doing the driving.

See also: ACCIDENT; CAR; JOURNEY

DROWNING   *Feeling helpless in deep water*

As a dream symbol deep water usually symbolises the great depth of your emotions, including your sexual feelings, and if you are out of your depth and in danger of drowning, the implication seems fairly obvious. It implies that your emotions are becoming overpowering, and you need to step back and take an objective view of your life situation. If water is merely one symbol among many in the dream, and especially if there is a narrative, or series of dream incidents leading up to immersion in water or danger involving deep water, the dream will probably need personal interpretation, taking all the factors into careful consideration. A *Dream diagram* may help in this.

See also: TIDAL WAVE; WATER

DUNGEON   *A dark lock-up*

The dream dungeon is liable to be part of yourself – your own *Personal unconscious mind*, in which case, anything it contains will belong to you. Your *Personal shadow* may lurk inside your dream dungeon, and this frightening figure is composed of all the factors you have refused to face during your normal everyday life. If you are yourself a prisoner in the dream dungeon, the implication is that you are feeling trapped by your own contents. You could explore the hidden side of your personality, by thinking back through your life.

See also: CAVE; CELLAR; PIT

DUST

Dirt tends to be acquired from outside of your surroundings. Dust tends to be made up of fine particles eroded from those surroundings, and which have settled over the years. It may even be flakes of your own skin. Dream dust tends to imply that you have been neglecting everyday values, becoming hide-bound perhaps, overlooking the things other people may find important. These factors need thinking round carefully. Dust builds up to the point where it may be difficult to breathe, and if you have experienced some real-life incident which involved lots of dust, this may well feature unpleasantly in your dreams. This is one type of situation wherein a *Lucid dream* will be helpful. Let the dust blow away!

See also: BROOM; DIRT; EXCREMENT

E

EAGLE *A Large bird of prey*

A very ancient dream symbol, a pre-civilization image of power, majesty, cruelty and wildness, supremacy, mastery of environment, keen eyesight, and pride. A dream eagle may symbolise any of these things and more in an abstract sense, or perhaps a person who somewhat resembles an eagle in looks and characteristics, and the influence such a person may be having on the dreamer. In America the bald eagle in particular can symbolise patriotism and the quality of being American. All the supposed qualities possessed by large birds of prey may be represented by their appearance in a dream, but individually one's own ideas and experiences will decide the significance to be attached to a dream eagle.

See also: BIRDS

EARTH MOTHER *The world and its characteristics represented by a human-type figure*

A personification of the planet on which we all live, the concept of the Earth Mother is closely associated with the concept of the *World dream*. She is everybody's mother, and she nourishes and cares for us all; everybody will have their own image of her, hidden in their subconscious mind and liable to emerge in dreams when aroused by some *Trigger event*. Despite her common inheritance, to become aware of this great supernatural mother goddess in dreams is a wholly personal event, and may reflect the beginning of the type of spiritual awareness that can mature into a quest for spiritual reality on a universal scale.

See also: GODDESS

EARTHQUAKE

When the familiar solid earth suddenly shakes, it shows that you can no longer rely on the stability of something you had thought unquestionably reliable. You may of course have experienced violent earthquakes yourself and the symbol will have become reality in your life, a premonition perhaps, of trouble ahead. But if not, its meaning will be perfectly plain: the only question is, what does the 'earth' represent to you exactly? It could be your family, or your place of employment, or some other institution on which you have been relying, or society's attitude towards you personally, or your health, or wealth. If it is any of these things you will probably know the answer. If not, the shaking 'earth' might represent materiality itself: a dream earthquake could be hinting at the temporary nature of life, and the possibility of coming to spiritual awareness, to seek broader horizons and new worlds.

See also: VOLCANO

EATING

Anything you imbibe may be symbolised in a dream as eating; not only actual food, but information and impressions as well. If the dream is pointing out that you are taking something into yourself, it will probably refer to something previously unsuspected, and possibly something which may do you harm. If actual food is featured, try to identify this and think about it carefully: you may be making yourself ill by eating something that is bad for you: perhaps some of the ingredients or cooking methods need changing. But all the other features and characters in the dream need looking at very carefully: they may seem to have nothing to do with actual food but relate to influences that are affecting you negatively, which only you, the dreamer, can interpret.

See also: BREAD; FEAST; FOOD

ECHO

If your voice is echoing in the dream

In ancient Greek myth the nymph Echo fell in love with the vain youth Narcissus, and when she finally realized that he loved no-one but himself, she pined away until only her voice remained. This is the prior meaning of an echo as a symbol: unrequited feelings, loneliness, a sense of hopelessness of purpose. Perhaps you are pitting yourself against an uncaring world, and the reply you hoped for does not seem to be forthcoming.

If the echo is caused by others

Memories lingering, the words remaining when the person has gone. If this featured in your dream, try to recall the emotions you felt at the time or on waking. Were these feelings pleasant or unpleasant? You may know who or what was the source of the echo. Are you echoing someone else's words, or trying to shake off the memories you would rather forget? Only you, the dreamer, can know the answer.

See also: LOST

ECLIPSE *The earth's shadow*

A solar eclipse

The sun must be one of the most ancient of symbols, the giver and keeper of life, the source of energy, and symbolic representative of spiritual powers. When the sun's light and heat is withdrawn, the implication is that some of these qualities are being withdrawn. Career prospects and financial affairs are symbolised by the sun, and the earth symbolises materiality and the burden of fate. When the earth's shadow covers the sun it suggests that one's source of income, comfort and security are in danger of being depleted in some way.

A lunar eclipse

The moon, an equally ancient symbol, is more personal and more 'material' symbolically than the sun, and relates to emotions and physical welfare. In a dream, when the earth's shadow falls across the moon giving it the dark reddish appearance of a lunar eclipse, romance and health are the probable issue. The dream may simply be expressing your own fears in these areas, but it may also carry the practical meaning of problems with the heart and circulation, or relating to the menstrual pause.

See also: DARKNESS; MOON; SUN

EGGS

A potent symbol of new life, of the imminent emergence of a new life form, of new growth, of the spring of the year, of Easter, and of rebirth after death. Eggs may also symbolise sex as being at the root of all creation, and may represent erogenous zones of the human body when the dreamer does not wish to be more specific for whatever reason. To dream of broken eggs implies that the hoped-for outcome of an enterprise will not be forthcoming. As always, the full contents and context of a dream featuring eggs should be explored for personal meanings, and only the dreamer can do this successfully.

See also: EMBRYO

Ego overruled in a dream

Words which describe the various facets of the human psyche may be used in slightly different ways by different people, and there is probably a deal of confusion regarding the word 'ego'. In this context, it is used to mean the conscious, wide-awake part of the personality which is concerned with oneself as an individual, the part of oneself that wishes, desires, contrives and thinks. It is the seat of the 'passions' and likes to think 'I do it my way!' The ego is of course absolutely essential for normal everyday living and getting on in the world, but when the body sleeps, the ego should sleep too. When we dream, the ego should not be involved in the process. As soon as we wake, the memory of the dream transfers itself to the ego, and sometimes the ego rejects the memory as so much nonsense. This is the reason people with powerful egos tend to forget their dreams. But the whole purpose of dreams is to present abstract issues without interference by the ego: when we sleep, the ego should be overruled by the *Inner feelings*. When we experience a *Lucid dream* the ego has refused to 'lie down' and tries to take over the dreaming process. This is rarely a good thing, because the whole point of dreams – recycling the thoughts and experiences of the day and re-presenting them in a digestible form – is thereby lost.

See also: Spherical symbolisation of the self

ELEPHANT

Usually amiable, potentially terribly dangerous; their great size and slow movements make them ponderous and impressive, rather like some official organizations. A dream elephant may well represent something like this, particularly if the dreamer has in some way fallen foul of authority. A man whose affairs were being investigated by the Income Tax authorities dreamed that a large and dangerous-looking elephant was peering in through his windows. But the elephant in your dream may also represent a person known to you and who is not unfriendly – a caricature of somebody with rather similar elephantine characteristics.

See also: ANIMALS

EMBROIDERY   *Needlework, tapestry or stitch-craft*

If you are embroidering in the dream

In the same vein as painting a picture, you are creating something that is not really there, or is not necessarily exactly as you are depicting it. It could be that you are deceiving someone – probably without ill-intent – and 'embroidering the truth' a little to make it appear more acceptable. Perhaps you have been explaining something complicated, and this is how your dream represents it.

THE KEY TO DREAM ANALYSIS

If the work has been done by someone else

The whole of nature has often been described as a 'tapestry' of innumerable life forms, and the dream image of a completed or half-formed tapestry could be expressing this, and the way in which you or something which has been occupying your attention fit into the scheme of things. Plainly a complicated situation is being symbolised. Could it be a 'tapestry of lies'?

See also: ART; PAINTING

EMBRYO

As a dream symbol this could be an unseen 'thing' about to emerge, or perhaps a chrysalis, or a hatching egg. The embryo is something new that is taking shape, whether it be solid and tangible or purely abstract, as an idea. Take careful note of your feelings when interpreting the dream, as these will give you an indication of whether the emergent entity is good or bad, wanted or unwanted. It is a favourite theme of Sci-fi stories, an innocent-looking 'embryo' which develops into a dangerous alien creature, and this idea may well influence the *Personal unconscious* when imminent danger is suspected. Even when the potential is desirable, the embryo itself may fail to develop and be aborted, with the implication that an idea that may have seemed brilliant and promising has not fulfilled its promise.

See also: EGGS

Enacting dreams in company

If you are with a group of others interested in interpreting their dreams, you can organize the details of your dream into a play involving other people taking the part of dream characters. It sometimes happens that the deeper meanings of the dream spring to mind as the play unfolds. The method is particularly useful in the case of long, convoluted dreams. All the 'actors' can give you their own interpretation of the parts they are playing. This is a party game with a really useful potential, but it has its limitations, and if you are at all a 'private person' you may be tempted to alter or gloss over the more embarrassing details, and reach a false conclusion. Perhaps the most constructive results are obtained in the case of children's dreams, in a family environment or at a party including the child's friends.

Encouraging dreams

It is important to allow the dream to have its say without interference by the conscious ego. But it may be that you have experienced a frustratingly inconclusive dream and feel sure that a further dream, a sequel or extension of the first, would give you a satisfying answer. The way to encourage this to happen is to quieten your thoughts and emotions when you are ready for sleep. You are already aware of the need and the potential, and there is no need to amplify this. Feel that there is an empty space in your own psyche, a space which is waiting to be filled by a dream. Your *Inner feelings* will already know of the need, ahead of your conscious mind. In quietness you are *asking* yourself for the required dream; if you try to *tell* yourself by being too vehement about it, the result may be a *Lucid dream* or a *Wish-fulfilment* dream which is liable to give you false or misleading answers.

Endo-psychic censor

In explaining the process by which thoughts, emotions and experiences, and in particular those matters which have been rejected by the conscious mind, become converted into symbols to emerge in due course as dreams, Sigmund Freud formulated the existence of a built-in censor whose function it was to disguise the form of anything which the conscious mind found distasteful. He termed this the 'endo-psychic censor', visualizing it as a psychic force able to modify anything incompatible with the dreamer's conscious self-opinion. In effect it was able to produce a cartoon picture out of a real situation, making it less offensive and thus more acceptable to the waking mind. You can understand the significance of a political cartoon only if you know something about the people and events to which it refers, otherwise it will remain merely an amusing drawing. He had noticed that a person might relate a dream without realizing its true meaning, and find it trivial or amusing. When they understood the true meaning however, they sometimes felt mortified. The purpose of the endo-psychic censor, he claimed, was to allow the dreamer to find some relief from repressed matters that had become troublesome, without causing distress to the waking mind.

See also: Freudian dreams

ENEMY   *A cause for defensive action*

The term 'enemy' might cover many types of dream experience. We speak of an *Assailant* when we mean somebody or something from outside of ourselves that seems to be opposing us in some way; and we speak of an *Adversary* to mean a hidden part of our own psychic contents that has become personified as an *Opponent*. An enemy may represent a real threat from a real person, or it too may be a personification of an inward problem that is becoming troublesome. It largely depends on the understanding of the person concerned, and the full context of the dream needs to be carefully analysed to find out what the problem is, and whether defensive action is required or if the problem lies in your own understanding of the situation.

See also: XENOPHOBIA

ESCAPING

If you are escaping in the dream

It is a fairly common dream experience, to be running away from something, someone, some kind of confrontation. If you are hiding from something, the cause needs to be identified and put into perspective. There may well be a real-life situation from which you feel the need to withdraw, and if this is the case the dream needs studying carefully to see if it contains any useful clues. If there is no obvious reason to escape, it may be that the dreamer is feeling stressed and could do with some time off, to 'get away from it all'.

If someone else is escaping from you

The symbol is certainly plain, and there should be a fairly obvious real-life situation which has triggered the dream. If there seems to be no such state of affairs, the escape has to be purely an abstract situation. It could be an outmoded or incorrect idea or attitude which you would be better off without. Why should anyone want to run away from you? the whole dream should provide the clue. You may have hurt someone's feelings inadvertently or upset someone's peace of mind.

See also: FUGITIVE

Evening dreams

If you have studied the *Cycle of the dreaming self* and the *Development of dreams*, you will appreciate the cyclic process that is continuously functioning beneath the threshold of awareness. You may not have regular sleeping habits, you may work at night and sleep during the day, in which case the term 'evening dream' will refer to dreams that happen soon after you fall asleep. Should you wake at this point the chances are that in your memory the dream will seem chaotic and meaningless. This is because the *Inner feelings* have not yet had a chance to do their work. As the night – or your period of sleep – progresses, remembered dreams will be that much more meaningful.

See also: Dozing dreams

Everyday dreams

This is a term which describes dreams which seem to make sense, and which deal with everyday events: confrontations with friends and colleagues, and general relationships. These are the dreams that may well contain psychological truths and hints concerning in particular relationships with other people. Some dreamers report long and convoluted dreams of this nature. Perhaps ninety percent of your dreams will fall into this category, and this book is not being dismissive. But the fact is that everyday dreams are likely to be well covered by all the facts and symbols listed here. Always refer back to the sections on analysing and recording your dreams, and on the use of dream diagrams and drawings. Then follow through by studying the possible meanings of everything that played a part in your dream. If you study the *Cycle of creation in dreams*, and the *World dream*, you will see that these belong to the psychic or spiritual level of materiality. This is no bad thing, but when you study and record your dreams you are likely to begin experiencing dreams which reflect a 'higher' spiritual level, perhaps culminating in dreams of the *Collective unconscious,* or even the *Human world of spirit*. Never overlook the basic symbols referring to the personal unconscious mind, and don't forget to read the entries relating to Adler, Freud and Jung, as these may give you valuable clues.

See also: Animal-nature dreams; Plant-nature dreams

EXAMINATION   *Being tested for knowledge*

It is a fairly common dream experience, to approach some subject, some project needing your expertise, with confidence, only to find to your dismay that you know nothing about it and are unable to answer any questions. There may not be any parallel in real life that you can think of, but the dream will probably be referring to a completely abstract 'exam'. You have been over-confident, too sure that you know the answers, but in what context? A variation of this theme is to dream that you are about to deliver a lecture on some subject about which you are confident, only to discover too late that you know nothing about it. A careful analysis of all the dream details may provide the clue: it could be referring to work, or to marriage. Exams are personal, individual things. The dream could be telling you to share your confidences, confide your problems and your worries, and not try to take too many responsibilities on your own shoulders.

See also: JUDGE

THE KEY TO DREAM ANALYSIS

Exasperation *(A theme mood)*

In real life when we become exasperated at some person or any tricky situation that you feel has been caused by somebody's negligence, it is usually because we have been expecting too much of the people concerned and are being unrealistic. People are as they are, you can't change them, and if they annoy you it might be best to avoid the sort of situation where confrontation will ensue. The situation is the same in dreams, and the implication is that you have been expecting too much of whatever or whoever you are finding exasperating. The dream may be telling you to be more broad minded and easygoing. It is no use trying to control other people's lives.

EXCREMENT

Human excrement in a dream symbolises faults and undesirable features that you need get rid of. In fact, the implication is that these factors have already come out of your body – your mind, your psyche – but by the nature of excrement which clings where it touches, you may be finding it very difficult to discard these things completely. 'The sow that was washed rolls in the mud again', and, like a bad habit that will not go away, memories cling. The whole dream needs analysing very thoroughly for clues, and if you can identify the nature of the dream excrement you will certainly benefit from the knowledge. Animal excrement can feature in dreams too, and may be pointing out that your affections are being misplaced in some direction. Time to be realistic!

See also: DIRT; DUST; TOILET

F

FACADE   *A false front*

Buildings often have facades – a built-up front wall perhaps to make the place look more impressive, or to fit in better with its surroundings. People are often much the same, putting on a false front for the benefit of others. In dreams a false front such as this is a common situation involving the *Persona*, and the *Self* is often symbolised in dreams as a building of some sort. If the building represents a real person, the dream is showing you that the person is putting on a false front in public, and of course that person might be you! Sometimes the opposite is the case – a building (or a person) is made to look less impressive, less significant than it really is, camouflaged, a case perhaps of 'inverted snobbery'. In both cases the dream is telling the dreamer something that could turn out to be very useful to him or her. There are numerous permutations of this dream symbol, and your personal interpretation is essential.

See also: ACTING; ART; PAINTING; THEATRE

FACTORY   *A place where things are manufactured*

This dream symbol may of course refer to a real place of work and feature in an *Everyday dream*, but on a larger scale it represents the power of materiality itself – the source of worldly wealth and normal social interaction.

If you dream you are outside of a factory looking in

There may be a *Theme mood* that will give you a clue. When you saw the factory did you feel that it was a good place to be, or somewhere to be avoided? This will reflect your own current attitude towards the hurly-burly of everyday life: you might want to join it, or escape it. The dream is offering you a look into your own self. You may perhaps be lacking in social confidence, with a feeling of 'them and us' with yourself as the outsider.

THE KEY TO DREAM ANALYSIS

If you are inside the factory and taking part

The dream factory may be an attractive place for you to be, or it may be somewhere you would dearly like to escape by retiring from the daily routine. This will reflect your attitude towards the society in which you live and work. Factories normally produce things: did these products feature strongly in the dream? They are the products of materiality, and if you found them unattractive in the dream, this could be reflecting your desire to seek a higher purpose in life.

See also: MACHINERY

FALLING

The sensation of falling is a common dream experience, sometimes happening without any dream images or symbols to support it. Some scientists suggest that the feeling harks back to the days when, like chimpanzees, humans are supposed to have made themselves sleeping-nests in trees, when falling would have been a very real danger. As an even older symbol it could reflect the *Cycle of creation* and the *World dream*, serving to anchor the *Inner feelings* firmly to the material world rather than reaching unrealistic heights of fantasy during the formation of dreams. But at all events the sensation certainly implies that the foundation or attitude of mind that you have been relying on is not quite so secure and solid as you had supposed. Usually, when we experience the sensation of falling, we wake up before we 'hit the bottom'. It would be interesting to stay asleep and experience the conclusion of the fall: whatever the outcome, it will already be a part of your own psyche and can do you no real harm. Identifying the nature and outcome of the fall may have lasting benefits on your waking life.

See also: Lucid dreams; Materiality; Nightmares

THE KEY TO DREAM ANALYSIS

Family-intuitive dreams

Family experiences can be shared by way of dreams, and it probably happens far more frequently than we realize. Children may relive or even pre-experience their parents' experiences. Parents may dream of their children's real-life problems – sometimes in symbolic terms, sometimes as straight-forward factual images, experiencing real incidents. Any such incidents are usually of a traumatic or unpleasant nature. Shared dreams have this quality: pleasant experiences do not call for sympathy; unpleasant ones do, and the more sympathy that exists in the relationship, the more a person is able to feel compassion rather than mere 'solidarity', the more often will such dreams occur. In a few cases, fear rather than sympathy may provide the intuitive link, possibly reflecting an abusive situation.

See also: Children's dreams; Dreams of other lives; Intuitive dreams

FARM

A farm is a practical place where crops and animals are reared, and anyone with farming experience may dream of a farm as an everyday background to their dream incidents. A dream farm is a 'virtual place' within the self where life-principles and soul-contents may be nurtured, abstract matters rather than anything with material or financial expectations. A dream *Baby* may represent an aspect of the *Self* coming newly to awareness, and a dream farm may represent the place where this child of the psyche is being reared: in other words, the farm can be a symbol of your own self. If this is the case in your own dream, try to recall any features and characters connected with the farm: they may represent important aspects of your own inner self which ought to be acknowledged.

See also: ANIMALS; CHILD; ZOO

FASHIONS   *To follow the current trends*

Style of clothes

As a dream symbol your *Clothes* represent your outward personality and the impression you give or would like to give to others. It follows that if you seek to wear the same as others of your set, or perhaps of people you admire, or young people, or forward-looking people, then you are trying to be accepted as one of them and do not wish to stand out as different. Perhaps in your dream you are admiring current fashions but cannot match them, and the implication is that you are falling short of the ideal, in your own eyes at least. Possibly the other dream characters may be slaves to fashion but you are proud to be different in this respect, and this reflects your attitude in real life: you refuse to go along with the crowd and prefer to think of yourself as unique.

Fashions in other respects

Fashions change continually, reflecting the normal tastes of the day. Perhaps you fear appearing old-fashioned, or possibly you want to stay out of the rat-race and refuse to go along with the latest gimmicks. In either case what happens in your dreams reflects your feelings in real life. You may be gazing wistfully at the possessions and lifestyles of others, and feeling left out of things; or perhaps you may be constantly involved in a race to 'keep up with the Joneses'. Dreams of this nature quite accurately portray your position in society as it is, and as you would like it to be.

See also: HAT; NAKED; UNIFORM

Fearfulness   *(A theme mood)*

A dream during which you experience fear is not really the same as a *Nightmare*, and fearfulness is not really the same as fear itself. You are fearful lest something might happen, that some feared outcome should ensue, that a situation might become dangerous. The dream may reflect a real-life situation which you recognize, but if not, it may be telling you to have more confidence in your own ability to deal with crises as they may arise. If you have a guilty conscience and justifiably feel concerned lest your guilt should become known, this dream may well be an admonishment. The hidden *Inner feelings* will let you know by way of dreams if you need to do something to assuage your feelings of guilt. If you have genuine concerns in real life, examine your dream very carefully for helpful clues.

See also: ADVERSARY; ASSAILANT

FEAST

Ordinary *Food* or the mere act of *Eating* is a dream symbol of taking in – and it may refer to information, impressions, learning, mental or even spiritual sustenance rather than actual food – but feasting certainly implies a degree of self-indulgence. The details of the dream are important, and so are the emotions which you may have felt during the dream or immediately after waking. If you felt rather guilty during your feast, perhaps you are being greedy or selfish in some respect. But if you felt only pleasure, and particularly if others were sharing your feast. it could be that you are set to receive some good fortune or a happy occasion, perhaps a family reunion.

See also: BREAD

FEET

Rather like *Driving* a car, feet symbolise one's progress through life, and the state of your feet in the dream may carry implications about your own attitude, your relationship with others, and the problems you encounter along the way. To dream you have deformed or damaged feet implies that you are experiencing difficulties in the normal course of events, but feet usually have a spiritual connotation in a dream: the journey they symbolise is the march towards psychic wholeness which is represented in numerous different ways both in psychoanalysis and in the religions of the world. To understand the importance of this symbol is an important step along this path. If the dream carries a hint of 'treading on somebody's toes' or harming others in some way, take it as a stern warning to live and let live. Studying and recording your dreams in detail is one way to become more aware of life's spiritual journey.

See also: PATH; LAMENESS; ROAD

FENCE

A dream fence is less final, less impelling, than a *Wall*. Both are barriers, but you can often see through a fence whilst a wall is solid and hides what is beyond it. The barrier may be physical, mental, moral, psychological, or spiritual, but you can usually 'see' beyond the barrier and understand what lies beyond it. The fence may be there for your own good, certainly for your own guidance, and it may direct you towards a safer path. To dream that a fence has fallen or blown down implies that a way which was formerly closed to you has now been opened. Only you can interpret the full meaning of the dream.

See also: GATEWAY; HEDGE

FISH or FISHING

The *Collective unconscious* has often been described as a vast sea full of archetypal images, and it is quite understandable that the desires, hopes and fears of the human race are often symbolised as creatures which live in this largely unexplored sea, for once these things enter the unconscious part of the mind, by definition they will have disappeared from consciousness, but still they live on, unseen and usually unsuspected. This is not merely an imaginative way to speak of forgotten matters that may suddenly be recalled to mind: it is much deeper and more significant than that. On a more personal scale the sea may symbolise one's depths of emotion, including sexual feelings. So may a lake, a river or a brook, and the creatures which live in it will be the emotional matters that we do not wish to recall, perhaps things we feel guilty about, or found too disturbing even to ponder over. The dream image of fishing – either by you personally, or as a spectator – expresses your own wish to enter this unconscious world, to uncover your own contents, and set out on a journey, both psychological and spiritual, which will change your life for ever. On a more practical level, perhaps, it can symbolise a wish to uncover your past, particularly if you have recently acquired an interest in your ancestry and family history.

See also: ANIMALS; *Personal unconscious mind;* SEA; WATER

FLOWER

This is a multi-faceted symbol when it appears in a dream, as it can refer to several different principles The whole dream needs analysing very thoroughly: are the dream flowers real flowers, or archetypal ones? If real ones, there may have been recent *Trigger events*. In archetypal terms the *Persona* or social mask that you wear can be dreamt of as a flower, or a vase of flowers, because obviously you want to be seen as an attractive person. A solitary flower can be a *Mandala* of the self – a picture perhaps of your own soul. A five-petalled flower as a mandala may be showing you the five personal passions common to everyone: the passions of 'observation', 'acquisition', 'aggression', 'attraction', and 'compassion', five petals surrounding the centre of the flower which is your own *Self.* A flower such as a water lily floating on water can symbolise you conscious self growing above the unfathomable contents of the unconscious mind. Emotional and sexual encounters may be symbolised by beautiful and exotic flowers. Flowers and flower-grown meadows often feature in 'death' dreams of the afterlife, and in this will reflect the *World dream*. On a more down-to-earth level, faded flowers may represent unfulfilled hopes and disappointments, while flourishing blooms express the hope of good times ahead.

See also: FOREST; LILIES

FLYING

As a rule dream images are selected and presented by the *Inner feelings*, and these hidden feelings, also known as the 'higher emotional centre' do not feel themselves to be bound by materiality or by the physical body in the way that your everyday feelings are. There is nothing to stop them flying around freely, and time and space are no real barriers to them. It sometimes happens that in your dream you seem to have two bodies, one heavy and earth-bound, the other light and able to fly: this is the distinction between these two modes of feeling, the material and the non-material. Ordinary dreams of flying in a plane, or perhaps hang-gliding and looking down over the world, can reflect a feeling of superiority, and this superiority may be either real or purely 'wishful'. Airliners in a dream are likely to carry the practical significance of travel, perhaps in anticipation of a relaxing holiday, or of someone or something having just arrived into your awareness.

See also: GLIDER

FOG *Heavy mist obscuring your view*

When a situation is uncertain and rather worrying, your dreams are likely to involve mist or fog to represent these negative feelings. The implication is that you cannot see any better way forward at present, and patience is necessary. Real fog often accumulates in low-lying place such as valleys, and the valley itself will represent the material situation that you find yourself in – your circumstances, your health, your career prospects. It also accumulates over water, and this fog may be referring to your emotional problems and your sex-life. Real fog lifts before long, and the implication of the dream may be that although you cannot see your way ahead clearly, the situation should improve before long. Sometimes you may dream you are standing on a hill and looking down at heavy fog or mist covering the plain and valleys beneath, and the implication seems to be that you have risen above, or are about to overcome your difficulties and should find a clear way ahead in future.

See also: CLOUDS; MIST; VALLEY

FOOD

The thoughts and impressions of the day are food for the unconscious mind to be digested through the night. Symbolically, all influences and any piece of information can be seen as food for the mind, for the emotions, for the psyche. In dreams there are endless permutations of the way in which abstract matters can be seen as food, and these possibilities need to be borne in mind when analysing your own dreams involving food. But of course the dream image of food can have a purely practical meaning too, particularly if you dream you are eating bad or stale food. This may be literally true if you are inadvertently using food that is bad for you.

See also: BREAD; FEAST; FRUIT

FORD *A shallow river crossing*

In dreams a river or a stream symbolises the flow of emotions, including the sexual desires, and these psychological forces can seem overpowering. You may be happy to swim in the river, to submerse yourself in the current of feelings; you may wish to keep aloof from these things during some encounter in your life, and you will look for a bridge enabling you to cross safely; but you may wish to 'test the water', to paddle through the river sampling the experience without becoming too involved, and a ford will symbolise this. If you are following a spiritual path you will sooner or later need to cross the dream river to become independent of these potent life forces.

See also: BRIDGE; PATH; RIVER; ROAD; WATER

FOREST

You may of course live in a forest, or have a background of forest life, and to dream of a forest may be simply setting the scene for you. But if not, a dream forest usually symbolises the mind – the 'forest of the mind' – when your thoughts are keeping you from seeing broader possibilities. The world with all its opportunities is not confined to your own ideas, your own preconceptions, and to walk through a dream forest seems to be telling you to look beyond the trees, to quieten your own thoughts and look for opportunities that may not seem logical or scientific. Many great thinkers are hampered by their own power of reason which can shut off higher possibilities for them, and they are then apt to dream of walking through a forest. In the *World dream* too forests are significant, and tend to represent aggression and the search for power.

See also: *Adlerian dreams;* AUTUMN; HEDGE

FORTRESS

If you are outside the fortress trying to get in

A fortress represents security – or apparent security – and if you are trying to get in, plainly you are searching for security in one way or another. Marriage is often symbolised in dreams by a fortress, or a strong tower, and this may be the implication in your dream. You will probably feel weak and helpless outside the fortress. Remember if anyone known to you featured in the dream, for they will provide the key to its interpretation.

If you are inside the fortress, looking out

All the features that tend to isolate the individual can be symbolised by a fortress, and it may be that you the dreamer have been feeling unsociable for whatever reason. You may suspect danger outside and are clinging to the security of your 'fortress'; or you may perhaps feel trapped in the fortress and would like to escape. If you can recall a *Theme mood* this will help your interpretation of the dream. It is an unequivocal symbol and the dreamer will probably know what it means and what needs to be done about it.

See also: *Adlerian dreams;*   BATTLEMENTS; FUGITIVE

FOSSILS

Ancient life-forms that no longer live but have come to light unexpectedly. Past thoughts and impressions that were rejected and forgotten but have suddenly come to the awareness again – your *Inner feelings* may have made this connection in your dream. Whatever else follows the discovery of a fossil in your dream will probably recapture the 'meat' of that long-dead creature, and the long-forgotten ideas, impressions or information that were relegated to the unconscious mind. These things will not simply disappear, and need your waking attention.

See also: ANTIQUE; ARCHAEOLOGY; *Personal unconscious mind*

FOUNTAIN

The ancient symbol of water gushing out of the ground signifies something new which has come to awareness, a new source of knowledge, or an unsuspected reason to feel great emotion, or perhaps a new surge of sexual attraction. It could relate to new birth, or a new and exciting discovery relating to society, business, religion, art or music. It is such a clear symbol that the dreamer will probably know immediately to what it refers.

See also: WATER

Free association

This is a psychological game that psychiatrists may use to try to locate problem areas in a person's mind. 'Say the word that springs to mind' in response to another word: there are always obvious examples, such as 'black – white', 'big – little', 'sky – blue' and so on, but the method can be very useful when trying to interpret your dreams. Take a feature in the dream that seemed to be important: what does it remind you of? And what does *that* word remind you of? And so on until you run out of possibilities. If you find that you hesitate before giving the obvious word, if you reject the first word you think of and choose another better one, if you start feeling uncomfortable about where the associations are leading – these are powerful hints that there is a problem area in your own psyche which has triggered the dream. It needs to be exposed, and complete honesty is needed. It may be best to play this game on your own rather than recruit a helper, because the presence of another person – however familiar and close – may inhibit the flow of associations.

Freudian dreams

Sigmund Freud was the pioneer who first explored the unconscious mind, and who realized that 'the interpretation of dreams is the royal road to knowledge of the unconscious activities of the mind'. He realized that only the individual can truly explore the recesses of his or her own unconscious mind, and that exploration of this nature can bring about a new dimension of life and a new-found confidence. Freud seemed to be somewhat obsessed by the sexual content of dreams. Nowadays as a rule people's sexual lives and inclinations are very much in the open, but in Freud's lifetime this was not the case. Sexual desires tended to be suppressed and consequently repressed – that is, driven from the conscious awareness into the dark recesses of the *Personal unconscious*. Because of this he saw dreams as primarily sexual by nature, but presented in a disguised form so that the dreamer would not find them too upsetting or embarrassing. He formulated what he called the *Endo-psychic censor* as a part of the personal unconscious mind capable of doing this. The actual contents of dreams he divided into two categories: the manifest, and the latent. The former sets the scene in a way anyone can understand; the latter contains the true meaning of the dream in a cryptic form. Any dream with a disguised sexual content is usually called a 'Freudian dream'.

See also: Oedipus dreams

Frightening dreams

If the frightener is known to you in waking life

A real-life situation which has become alarming enough to feature in your dreams is very much a problem for you to face in waking life, although the dream itself may give you some clue as to the best course of action. An abstract situation may be just as much a real-life circumstance as a practical problem, but in this case it tends to reflect your own innermost contents. This kind of situation which you find an ongoing worry and is affecting your dreams may have taken on a form and shape of its own and could be called an *Assailant*. Particularly obscure worries may be narrowed down and identified by analysing your dream. Although the solution is probably to be found in your day-to-day activities, the dream itself may provide clues as to the best way to go about this, particularly if it has been a *Dawn dream*.

THE KEY TO DREAM ANALYSIS

If the frightener is completely unknown or 'demonic'

Having studied the nature of the *Personal unconscious mind* and the *Shadow*, you will know that psychological disturbances are usually caused by matters which have been rejected or ignored by the conscious mind, and have congregated beneath the *Inner feelings* to emerge perhaps in some frightening form during your dreams. If you study the details of the dream carefully, you will probably be able to identify the nature of this 'creature'. Sometimes if you have been dabbling in the occult you will experience something unpleasant when you decide to follow a more spiritual path. At all events, the frightening apparition is already a part of your own psyche and cannot harm you further – but it needs to be identified, coaxed out of its hiding place, and dispersed!

See also: ADVERSARY; DEMON; *Nightmares*

FROST

The atmosphere is the natural environment of us all, and water symbolises emotions: water in the atmosphere or dew which has frozen implies that your emotional surroundings and thence the attitudes of other people towards you have become distinctly frosty. There may be a good reason for this – only you, the dreamer, can know. There may be a difficult, slippery path to follow for a time. But frost is transient, and conditions should improve before long.

See also: GLACIER; SNOW AND ICE; WATER

FRUIT

The outcome of something is often symbolised by fruit: your new enterprise: will it 'bear fruit'? Your children, the 'fruit of your loins', will they achieve attractive ripeness, or shrivel up and wither? When they feature in a dream, fruits, and your children too, may symbolise your own ideas, hopes and ambitions. Fruit can also symbolise health, or healthy relations with others, particularly in physical terms. Things that resemble fruit in some way can also appear in dreams as actual fruits if they are attractive to the dreamer, and the phallic significance of bananas and the like is fairly obvious.

See also: FOOD

FUGITIVE *The outsider escaping or hiding*

Assuming that the dreamer has no real-life practical reason to evade capture and the dream is reflecting this unenviable situation – and possibly offering helpful clues – the symbol of running away, or of looking wistfully longing to join society is very expressive of the desire to achieve a more rewarding lifestyle. The implication is that the dreamer has been feeling left out of things, and would dearly like to be accepted on more equal terms. The context of this dream symbol will be entirely a private matter for the dreamer, and only he or she can interpret it successfully.

See also: ESCAPING; LOST

FUNERAL

Waking thoughts and fears of death may well produce a dream funeral. There is an example of this in the section on *Dream diagrams* which showed that such worries were unfounded. The symbol is not usually to be taken literally, however. The implication of a funeral is that some 'life' has come to an end, and this 'life' may be some abstract principle: it may relate to matters of work, society, a particular line of interest which is now over, a habit which has gone, a friendship which has been lost. The end of a bad period is the necessary precursor of better times ahead.

See also: BURIAL; DEATH

Future coming to awareness in dreams

Quite a few people long to be able to dream of the future, but this is not something to aim at. Dreams of the future happen quite frequently, but they are not to be controlled. They must come about not through the will, or the ego, but from the *Inner feelings* – the psychic compartment in us which has the ability to see ahead. These inner feelings work beneath the surface of awareness and normally remain there, and they are completely independent of the everyday heart and mind: they cannot be directed by the will. When people use their desires to try to 'conjure up' a dream giving them the answer to some problem, the result is likely to be what is known as a *Wish-fulfilment dream;* a dream which is really no more than the exercise of imagination. True dreams of the future, when they happen, are quite involuntary and almost always relate to wholly private matters divulged to the dreamer alone. Very often they relate to family members or close acquaintances and tell of future quarrels, illnesses, and similar traumatic incidents. They are not really concerned with world events, unless these will affect the dreamer personally.

G

GATEWAY

A door is a solid barrier that may be either open or closed. A dream gate is a way through; it may be closed, but you can see through it and in that sense you know what lies beyond it. You may wish to go through the gate; you may actually pass through it; or you may be aware of its presence but have no wish to go through to whatever you believe to be on the other side. As a dream symbol the act of passing through a gateway implies gaining a new way of thinking or looking or understanding.

See also: DOOR; FENCE; HEDGE; WALL

GHOST

An unseen or nebulous presence in a dream implies just that: something you suspect might have an effect on you; something that you cannot put your finger on. You are probably rather scared of its possibilities should it become solid and tangible. It may be allied to the principle of a 'skeleton in the cupboard', perhaps a family secret that you do not want to be made known. If you believe that a ghost lurks in an unseen place – perhaps in a cellar – the dream symbol is hinting at something, some problem or hidden characteristic perhaps, that is threatening to emerge from the recesses of your *Personal unconscious mind*. You may have been repressing some unpleasant truth or long-past incident that could cause trouble if exposed for all to see. A dream ghost is something at least half hidden, that you would prefer to remain completely out of sight.

See also: ADVERSARY; DEMON; *Shadow*

GIFT

If you are offering someone a gift in your dream

The implication is that you are offering an aspect of yourself to the other person, something that represents the way you would like them to see you. You may know the other person in real life, and their reaction to the gift will be very significant: they may be accepting or rejecting your friendship, your advice, your own opinion of yourself.

If you are being offered the gift

If the donor is known to you in waking life, the dream symbol should be plain. They are offering you something, not necessarily a material object, that may be of value to you, or it may be disappointing and rather unpleasant. Another person's advice tends to have this nature. The implication is the same if the dream character offering the gift is unknown to you: he or she may be an *Archetype of the unconscious mind*. If this is the case the dream gift will probably be of great value to you: an interesting dream symbol, but a wholly personal one.

See also: Persona; TREASURE

GLACIER

A solid, frozen river of ice: a dream symbol that probably reflects your own emotional attitude to others. Your emotions ought to be flowing freely, and your personal relationships should not be frigid. The symbol may also reflect the feelings of someone else close to you, in which case the outlook for future relationships is not good. There needs to be a warming of hearts.

See also: FROST; SNOW AND ICE

GLIDER   *Soaring above the ground*

You may be in the glider and looking down, or you may be on the ground and looking up at it. The former represents your own feelings experiencing a 'high', and the latter expresses the wish to leave earthly worries behind and float above them. In both cases, though the glider seems to be independent and free from the earth, in fact it is still bound by the laws of gravity – the life forces of materiality – and has to come down sooner or later. It may be a *Wish-fulfilment dream* in which the dreamer seeks to escape the bonds of society, work, and responsibilities.

See also: FLYING; *Inner feelings*

GODDESS

What exactly is a goddess, and what does one look like? The answer depends entirely on the dreamer's own understanding. He or she will know if the dream figure is truly a 'goddess'. She may be the *Earth mother* herself, and one of the *Archetypes of the unconscious mind*, but she will certainly have emerged from the unconscious mind of the dreamer. She may offer sound advice when it is most needed, or she may provide a first inkling of the true nature of the *World dream*. Purely on a psychological (that is, not a spiritual) level, a dream goddess can personify the principle of female confidence and power, and the dream details should make the meaning clear. Following the lead of the 'goddess within' can be overdone as a practical concept, leading to an unfeminine tendency to dominate people and situations.

See also: WISE PERSON; WITCH

GOLD

As the major symbol of wealth, gold can have two distinct and very different meanings: it can refer to the gold of the earth and material riches; or it may refer to the spiritual wealth that the concept of 'enlightenment' can bring. In dreams, important people may sometimes be identified by their golden robes, and this often applies to *Archetypes of the unconscious mind* when they appear in dreams ready to give good advice. To dream of finding gold or similar treasures is not always a good omen; it may refer to short-term gain leading to long-term disappointment.

See also: TREASURE

GORGE   *A deep cleft through solid rock*

If in your dream you are looking down at a gorge, or ravine

Solid earth and rocks form a very basic dream symbol referring to the strength of materiality itself, and a cleft in that solidity which you cannot or do not wish to enter is normally a symbol of one's own unconscious mind. If you fear falling in however, the implication could be a very practical one: you may be feeling in danger of losing security in some sense; losing your job perhaps, or feeling that your marriage is in jeopardy. It means that solid materiality is not as reliable as you have thought.

If in your dream you are inside and exploring the gorge

Perhaps you are trying to find a way out. This implies that you are feeling hemmed in by circumstances beyond your control. The dream image may be warning you to withdraw from a situation before it is too late. The gorge could represent the recesses of your *Personal unconscious mind*, particularly if you find yourself remembering disturbing images from the past which are liable to cause you problems. The gorge can also represent the female element of marriage when this is threatening to become overpowering in some way. Someone known to you in waking life may be exerting an unpleasant influence, and you need to appraise your current lifestyle very thoughtfully.

See also: ABYSS; *Yin and yang*

GRAVE

The dreamer will know if this is a straight-forward reference to a real grave. A visit to a family grave can carry all the implications of past relationships with the deceased person, and how they would have reacted to the dreamer's recent waking experiences. This is true in real life as well as in dreams. But if this kind of personal connection plainly does not apply, as a dream symbol a grave is likely to be pointing out the final outcome of a situation – whether it be a relationship, an enterprise, or a way of life. Perhaps a recent *Trigger event* has brought the dreamer's attention to the end of a personal era. This symbol may well represent an emotional aspect in the dreamer's life that has reached its logical conclusion and needs putting to rest. The grave can also symbolise the recesses of the *Personal unconscious mind* with all its hidden contents – drawing attention to something that needs bringing out into the light: a guilty secret perhaps?

See also: BURIAL; DEATH; FUNERAL

Great dreams

This is a term used to describe dreams which contain more than the usual type of contents, cryptic or otherwise. Such dreams draw on the *Collective unconscious* and even the *Spiritual world* to bring an important message. One is usually left in no doubt about the special nature of such dreams. They usually occur in the early dawn, at a time just prior to waking, when they are most likely to be remembered in detail, and they are always very vivid. The nature of the message or information they bring is entirely a personal matter, though it may relate to other people as well as the dreamer personally. A study of the *World dream* will show that these dreams represent something of great significance and value to the individual who experiences them.

See also: Dawn dreams

Group dream-therapy

Some people like to tell of their dreams and discuss them; others prefer to keep them private. A group of friends can be supportive and will always give their opinions, and offer their interpretations of dreams that can prove baffling to the individual. They can ask questions and point out connections that would otherwise elude the dreamer personally. But, recalling Freud's *Endo-psychic censor*, there will always be images cropping up in a dream that refer to matters the dreamer may prefer to keep private, and could prove embarrassing under these circumstances. Remember the old saying about 'washing one's dirty linen in public'!

H

HAT

The dream symbol of hats as worn by characters in a dream, or the dreamer personally, is closely allied to the symbol of *Clothes*, as they both express the nature and personality of the people wearing them, and their function in relation to the dreamer. This is true whether the dream characters are real people known to the dreamer, or *Archetypes of the unconscious mind*. In the case of the former, a hat might also represent the way in which the person would *like* to be seen, that is, their *Persona*. When the character wearing the hat is female, it is worth bearing in mind that in some cultures and religions, a woman is expected to wear a head-covering if she is not to be thought wanton or immoral. In this case a hat may be a symbol of virtue.

See also: FASHIONS

Hate   (A theme mood)

Whatever the subject matter of your dream, if the feeling of hatred accompanied it and stayed with you as you woke, it can represent a call for action on your part. Hate is a totally negative emotion which really has no legitimate place in the mind of a reasonable person. In a dream, whether the hatred is yours and directed towards somebody else, or whether other dream characters are projecting this unpleasantness at you, the root of it probably lies in your own conscience. The *Inner feelings* are the seat of conscience, and the hatred you feel is expressing a deep feeling of guilt on your own part. If you really do feel hatred towards another person, try to see life from their point of view. You may find that the hate you felt has turned to sympathy.

Healing dreams

The pioneer psycho-analysts Freud, Adler and Jung, each in their own way, thought of dreams as possessing a great healing potential, and certainly if remembered, recorded, followed and understood they can lead to the removal of much psychological clutter, resulting in a healthier psyche. Your own *Inner feelings* are well aware of your shortcoming, and are able to create dreams which seemed aimed specifically towards a healing process. These often include images such as an ambulance or a *Hospital*. But any dream that points out negative reactions and features unpleasant emotions will function as a healing dream, if the hint is taken by the dreamer. We all benefit from a positive attitude towards life, despite all its ups and downs.

HEDGE   *A barrier formed of living plants*

In effect, a narrow strip of woodland which encloses or divides or connects, forming a home for small creatures and a barrier for large ones, including humans. A dream hedge could be bearing flowers, a friendly hedge that will protect and guide your path; or it could be menacing, full of thorns, and a hindrance to your course through life. The *World dream* points out that plants may well symbolise aggression and struggle; but of course they are also peaceful, beautiful and useful. One cannot be dogmatic about the hedge as a dream symbol; your dream will tell you which role it is playing.

See also: FENCE; WALL

Helplessness   *(A theme mood)*

A feeling of helplessness pervading your dream usually relates to your own recent experiences. It could be called an *Adlerian dream*, reflecting a personal search for power and confidence, resulting from unfortunate real-life experiences. Depending on its contents a 'helpless' dream needs searching carefully to see if it offers any clues as to the best way forward.

HERO   *A character who may solve your problems*

The hero-figure in a dream is closely allied to the *Wise person* and the *King, Archetypes of the unconscious mind* who are really able to give you good advice, if you are willing to listen. It may equally be a dream heroine, and in this case the archetypes are likely to be the *Queen* or the *Goddess*. They are interested in your problems, because they are part of your own psyche – the highest part – and whatever your current course in life they are always ready to give a helping hand, particularly once you become aware of your dream life and are ready to accept their advice. The hero figure in your dream may, of course, be a real person known to you, and on whom you have been relying, and in this case his or her help may not be as useful as you had hoped.

Holistic understanding

The term implies accepting something – a person, a situation, a dream – as a whole without attempting to analyse this or that detail. The more 'advanced' a person is in spiritual terms, or the more psychologically 'individuated' they are, the more likely will they be to accept wholes rather than look at the details. The nature of analysis is to break down 'wholes' to discover what they are made of; but in human terms the 'whole' is more than merely the sum total of parts, and the more one analyses, the less likely one is to arrive at a holistic understanding. The basic reason for this is that spiritual matters cannot be analysed, because they lie beyond the scope of the human mind. Even the cleverest scientists, you might conclude, can never arrive at a holistic understanding while they rely on their own brain-power to achieve that understanding. But as this book points out, dreams cannot be understood with the mind if they are not first analysed for their meaning. The understanding itself has to arrive independently. Truly *Spiritual dreams* if and when they are experienced will not need analysis; and this book will then no longer be needed. In everyday life the term 'holistic' is used to mean taking every part of the person into account, both physical and psychical, as in 'holistic healing'.

HOLLY

A holly hedge like a hedge of thorns can provide a formidable barrier – a thorny problem – but holly has the added dimensions of colourful berry, modest white flower, and festive associations. Holly sometimes appears in a dream when a new enterprise is under consideration, and the implication is that, though rewards should follow, difficult circumstances will be very much to the fore. Holly is a cautionary symbol: something appears very attractive, but someone could get hurt.

See also: HEDGE; THORNS

HONEY

Since ancient times honey has been greatly valued as a luxury food to be obtained at some personal risk. As a dream symbol a wild bees' nest or a beehive or a honeycomb carry this message: some advantage is to be gained if one is willing to take the risk involved. A pot of honey in these modern times will probably have lost its 'sting' as a dream symbol, and for anyone who is not a bee-keeper will simply point to a sweet situation. The word 'honey' of course is often used as a term of affection with no connotation of danger: the connection between honey and bees in this case has probably been lost over the years.

See also: FOOD; INSECTS

Horror   *(A theme mood)*

This powerful emotion is not really the same as fear, and when it forms the background to your dream, or remains with you after you wake, it implies that you are aghast at what you have experienced. There are horror stories and horror movies which can affect anyone who watches them, but the horror in these cases arises from some imaginative situation outside of your own psyche; you are letting it in and experiencing it. But in a dream, the chances are that the horror you feel arises from inside of yourself: from the *Personal unconscious mind*. It will have arisen because of factors that you did not want to deal with while you were awake, perhaps matters that you refused even to consider. However, If there are real unpleasant circumstances in your life that will not leave you alone even when you sleep, study the details of the dream carefully. They may contain a clue about the best course of action for you to take.

HORSE

Horses feature in dreams surprisingly frequently, even when the dreamer has no connection with horses personally. If that connection is there, the dream horse will have a practical meaning, but if not, there is usually a sexual implication. A white horse which features in a dream is likely to represent a person whom you trust, but whose sexuality you are nervous about. A black horse may symbolise the sexuality of a person you find somewhat frightening: an unknown quantity; a 'dark horse'. If you are used to riding horses you will very likely be doing just that with the horse in your dream. Animal energy and stamina with great sexual capacity, naturally competitive, sometimes compliant, sometimes wild and untamed: there is always a powerful emotional overtone in dreams about horses. A unicorn, a horse with something extra, a horn, or perhaps a crown, expresses a spiritual element in addition to the more obvious sexual symbolism.

See also: ANIMALS

HOSPITAL

A place to be healed, obviously, but as a dream symbol a hospital is more likely to be concerned with the psyche than with the body. It may be that you are mistaken about something or somebody and have been judging them unfairly, and the hospital wants to 'cure' you of this; or you may have been feeling guilty about some feature or characteristic or habit which you would like to be rid of, and the dream hospital is reflecting this wish. If people you know in real life are involved, their roles in real life and their actions in the dream – and whatever else you know about them – will hold the key to the meaning of the dream.

See also: DOCTOR; *Healing dreams*

HOTEL *A place where people are being looked after*

A dream hotel is not necessarily a real building: it probably represents some set of circumstances, or the surroundings on which you have been relying. It might be an organization to which you belong, or a family environment, or a safe haven of some kind. You will probably know the real nature of the 'hotel'. It is quite a common dream circumstance to leave your 'hotel' and walk or drive away, only to find that you have become lost and caught up in unpleasant circumstances. This could be construed as a warning not to abandon some situation that has been beneficial to you in the past.

See also: FARM; FUGITIVE

HURRICANE *A cyclone, a gale, a typhoon, a whirlwind*

Just as a real storm disrupts the elements and causes damage, a storm in the dreamer's own psyche causes disruption and possible emotional trauma. The cause may well be known to the dreamer; there may have been a series of *Trigger events*, upsets in the family or at work. If there are no obvious clues that the dreamer can remember, this could be taken as a *Warning dream*. It might refer to emotional upsets, possibly with a medical basis, that are due to affect either the dreamer personally or someone close to them. It may be referring to public reactions to something the dreamer or a member of the family has brought about, especially if that person is already in the public eye. Of course, the possibility of a real hurricane happening should not be ruled out.

See also: EARTHQUAKE; TIDAL WAVE; VOLCANO

HUT *A small building, a shed or shack*

Dream buildings often symbolise the *Self*, and a small wooden building, a temporary shed scarcely large enough to hold more than one person at a time, tends to represent the individual who has become cut off emotionally in some way. If a person enters the hut in your dream, he or she is undergoing something that applies to them alone: they are on their own in every sense. It is quite often the symbol of illness or death. When the person emerges from the hut he or she will have become changed, and must seek or be shown a new direction, a new environment – for better or worse.

See also: BARN; DOOR

I

IDOL   *A symbol of something that is worshipped*

An idol symbolises a principle that is greater than either itself or its worshippers. As a dream symbol its meaning is bound to be wholly personal: what does it mean to you, the dreamer? What were your feelings during or immediately after the dream? Of reverence, or contempt, or fear? Did it feature strongly in a major dream, particularly if it was a *Dawn dream?* You need to explore your own feelings and understanding very carefully and sincerely. It could represent a step up for the dreamer, or a denunciation of something the dreamer was relying on, a letdown for the emotions. This is a very important dream symbol, and it needs thinking round very thoroughly.

See also: CARVINGS; STATUE

Impersonal dreams

Dreams of things and places, relationships, family, friends and colleagues, and even dreams of the dark horrors that are liable to emerge unbidden from the depths of the *Personal unconscious mind*, all these are *Personal dreams*. Impersonal dreams begin when we begin to record and interpret our dreams. They are likely to contain information about matters previously unknown; they may be reflections of the *World dream*, they will probably include images taken from the vast sea of the *Collective unconscious*. They may even be truly *Spiritual dreams*. Impersonal dreams seem to leave the restrictions of science and human learning behind and enter the realm of the miraculous, a place where true wisdom is to be acquired.

INCENSE

Religion, it has to be said, belongs to the heart. Spirituality belongs to the soul. When you first enter a truly spiritual path you may well experience ethereal incense – a non-physical smell that arises when coarse material characteristics are being expelled from the *Inner feelings*. Many years ago the process was thought of as 'casting out demons', and people tried to recapture this experience by burning various substances that they thought recalled the supernatural smell, and this is why incense is sometimes burnt during religious ceremonies. If the smell of incense features in a dream, depending on the other dream features, it implies that the dreamer or the characters using the incense are exercising faith and sincerity; anything to be understood from such a dream should be valued and respected.

See also: CHURCH; *Spiritual dreams*

Incubating dreams

This is a dream-worker's term for invoking a dream about a certain issue, or trying to make it happen by concentrating on the subject just before you go to sleep. It should be remembered that all dreams of any value arise from images selected by the hidden *Inner feelings*, and not from the ego, or from the everyday emotions, or the thinking part of the brain. A powerful ego can quite easily take the stage and overrule the deeper – or higher – aspects of your own psyche; if you *wish* for a dream, this is what will happen. If you try to *command* a dream, your everyday thinking mind will produce one for you. The result will be what is known as a *Wish-fulfilment dream* which will be of no use whatsoever. Think about any problems you may have, and *submit* them with a feeling of trust. Some dream-workers recommend writing these things down and 'posting' them under your pillow, but at all events it is important to subdue any strong desires you may have. Any kind of passionate commitment will have the negative effect of encouraging the conscious ego to intervene in the formation of any resultant dream. The inner feelings which are responsible for assembling your dreams (see below) do not need to be 'told' about the matter: they are already well aware of your needs.

Inner feelings

The 'higher emotional centre' or the emotional part of the *Personal unconscious mind* which sifts and categorizes all the actions, thoughts, impressions and emotions that have been mulled over, worried about, and perhaps rejected and ignored, by the conscious mind. It contains all these matters and far more, for it has access also to the *Collective unconscious* and is able to select dream images both personal and impersonal when these seem to summarize the dreamer's day-to-day experiences, and put them in their most telling perspective.

INSECTS *Running, crawling, creeping or flying bugs*

As distinct from parasitic bugs, the general term 'insects' covers a multitude of life-forms, including such creatures as spiders, which are not really insects at all. As a dream symbol, their meaning depends on what 'insects' mean to you personally. Some people find them repulsive; others take an interest in their lives and habits. If the former, they may reflect a problem of health and hygiene which you suspect exists, or perhaps a feeling of compromised security, when insects are getting in to your house. Any other clues in the dream need to be studied very carefully, because action on your part is probably urgently needed.

See also: ADVERSARY; ASSAILANT; BUGS

Interpreting dreams for others

It has often been said that only the dreamer personally can interpret a dream properly, because only he or she knows all the circumstances and life-experiences which have gone before. What we can all do for others, however, is to *analyse* a dream and point out its manifest content and the implications of the images involved. The latent content can only be hinted at.

See also: Analysing dreams; Endo-psychic censor

Inter-reactive dreams

Can two people be involved in the same dreaming process, and experience the same dream? You may discover that this does occasionally happen. The *Inner feelings* are aware of far more than their own immediate contents, and the *Collective intelligence* as its name implies can control the outcome and imagery of dreams for the benefit of more than one person at once. In the manner of an *Intuitive dream*, you may sometimes dream of someone else's experiences in accurate detail, particularly when there is some sort of emotional link between you and this other person. You may also dream of another person's hopes and fears, particularly perhaps their worries and upsets, for these are more easily shared than pleasant experiences. Dream inter-reaction depends to a great extent upon the individual's capacity to have sympathy, to empathize and feel compassion for the other person. Perhaps a certain amount of *Holistic understanding* is needed.

Intuitive dreams

This type of dream explores the same territory as the *Inter-reactive dreams* (*above*). Intuition is the understanding to be gained by empathizing with another person. When the *Inner feelings* are approaching awareness, that is, less *unconscious*, intuition becomes quite open, allowing the thoughts and feelings of one to be experienced by others. This characteristic is equally pronounced by way of dreams, and dreaming about the waking-life experiences of others, particularly perhaps of family and friends, becomes a common experience. It may be advisable at times to keep this type of dream stricty private and avoid leaving a written record. An honest experience of this nature could cause badly hurt feelings. There is a strong connection between this type of dream (of living people whom you know), and the so-called *Reincarnation dreams* (of dead people whom you did not know).

J

Jekyll and Hyde dreams

Sigmund Freud wrote of the Id – the dark side of ourselves – as opposed to the Super-ego, which is our conscientious side. When discussing dreams we can speak of the *Shadow* as the dark part of ourselves which has become repressed and hidden beneath the *Inner feelings*. In Robert Louis Stevenson's famous story, which he said had been prompted by one of his own dreams, he visualized this unpleasant side of the personality as Mr Hyde, coming to life in the night and taking over control from the good Dr Jekyll. When the shadow of the *Personal unconscious mind* becomes too burdensome it may balance out the *Persona*, and dreams are then liable to alternate between the two extremes: selfish attention-seeking on the one hand, and inflation or self-importance on the other. If a sequence of this sort is proving a worry, it is a good idea to seek a new balance favouring neither one nor the other. This can be done by quietening ones own thoughts and emotions immediately before sleeping, and adopting an attitude of submissive expectation. Doing this has the effect of broadening the possibilities of your dreams, and making them less personal.

JETTY   *An inroad into the sea*

Attaining access to the sea of emotion, or sexual desire, ready to board a boat to cross it safely, or perhaps to become washed away and lost in the flood: this is the implication of a dream jetty, a pier, a breakwater, or a causeway leading across the bay. The dreamer seems to be approaching a situation where these powerful feelings are rampant, and cannot decide whether to take part in them, to merely watch and wait, or to remain aloof without actually becoming involved. The sea always contains an element of danger, and it as well to identify your own dream sea, and the jetty which at present is supporting you. They will be very significant factors in your life.

See also: BRIDGE; STEPPING STONES; WATER

JEWELS

Pearls always symbolise a non-material treasure; gold can be either material or non-material; jewels or precious stones which have their origin in the ground almost always symbolise riches or advantages that arrive by materialistic rather than spiritual means. The key to a treasure-house may predict an upturn in business affairs.

See also: CRYSTALS; GOLD; PEARL; TREASURE

JOURNEY

If it is you taking a journey

The chances are your dream journey will probably refer to your normal progress through life, and will be pointing out and isolating incidents which happen to you along the way. Assuming you are not due to take a real-life journey, you can be sure it is an ongoing journey of the mind. Details may refer to your health, your work, your family relationships, and if it is possible to assemble the details of your dream journey in sequence, the resulting analysis may prove revealing.

If someone else is taking a journey, or arriving from a journey in your dream

The chances are that this dream is predicting events that will coincide with these people coming to your attention in real life, rather than the new arrivals themselves. Make a point of remembering the dream details and await results over the next few days.

See also: CAR; FEET; PATH; RAIL JOURNEY; ROAD

Joy (A theme mood)

It would be a pleasant dream indeed that is characterized by the feeling of joy. But dreams of spiritual significance which might be thought of as joyful are more likely to be characterized by the feeling of patience and submission rather than joy. A *Wish-fulfilment dream* may create the joy of achievement, which may well be short-lived. It sometimes happens that one awakes with a feeling similar to joy, after having a dream which, on reflection, has been about rather unpleasant things and unwelcome characteristics. This could be because the dreamer has been taking a perverse pleasure in matters that he or she would be better off without.

JUDGE

If you are making a judgment in the dream

It is always easy to judge somebody else's words and deeds, because everyone falls short of perfection. But the religious injunction to 'judge not lest ye be judged' is something to be taken seriously, because everything you do is recorded by your own conscience – your own *Inner feelings* – and your own soul, and sooner or later we all have to face the consequences. A dream of casting judgment would seem to be warning you to have an open mind about these matters.

If another person is sitting in judgment in your dream

If you are being judged in a dream the implication is that you are already feeling guilty about something you have done, either by word or deed. Your inner feelings are the seat of conscience, and they are telling your waking mind to be more careful in what you do or say; don't forget that words can be very hurtful, and inflicting injuries of this nature adds to your own burden in the form of your *Shadow* which may cause completely unforeseen problems.

See also: ANGEL; EXAMINATION

JUNCTION   *A dividing of the ways*

A dream which seems to offer you the choice of directions in your path through life will certainly be reflecting your real-life situation, either physically, mentally or emotionally. Like a crossroads, a dream junction shows that your present course cannot continue, and a change of attitude must be made. A point of decision featuring in your dream often announces the appearance of an unknown character who turns out to be one of the *Archetypes of the unconscious mind*. If this seems to be the case on waking, all the dream details need recalling very carefully because they are sure to include sound advice from the highest intuitive part of your own self.

Jungian dreams

Ordinary material dreams about everyday relationships and happenings, according to the *World dream* which affects us all, are related to the solid background, the rock and minerals, of the earth itself. *Adlerian dreams*, by the same token, are related to the life of plants which are constantly striving to attain a better hold on the earth. *Freudian dreams* reflect the sexual conflicts that we may experience from time to time, and in this are related to the animal nature of life on earth. Jungian dreams represent a leap forward from these categories, and relate to the life force that rightfully belongs to human beings. Carl Gustav Jung was interested in the psychological process which he called 'individuation', involving a gathering into the self of collective factors and assimilating that part of the psyche which is normally unconscious. This process is akin to the spiritual process of 'atonement'. He formulated the existence and characteristics of the various *Archetypes of the unconscious mind* which, he claimed, are the manifestation of collective factors common to all mankind, coming to individual awareness. Dreams which feature these archetypes, often invoking the higher intuitive powers of the psyche, and dreams which contain material that seems to have arisen from non-personal or collective sources, could be called Jungian dreams. Whilst describing the characteristics of archetypes which may come to awareness by way of dreams, Jung encouraged the people who consulted him to analyse and interpret their own dreams, ascribing great importance to the keeping of accurate dream records, and also to the making of drawings or paintings to bring out their meanings while still fresh in the memory. Jung of course, being a psycho-therapist, often found himself dealing with psychologically disturbed people. But there is

THE KEY TO DREAM ANALYSIS

certainly no need to become unbalanced or disturbed in order to reap the very real benefit of his acquired knowledge and wisdom. Even in the case of bafflingly complicated or obscure dreams, he said: 'If we meditate on a dream sufficiently long and thoroughly – if we take it about with us and turn it over and over – something almost always comes of it'.

K

KING *A very important, distinguished character in your dream*

If this is not a real person known to you

The king in this case is probably one of the *Archetypes of the unconscious mind* and represents a part of your own psyche that may have some important advice to impart. It is, perhaps, the seat of wisdom and accumulated knowledge. Think around all the details of the dream very carefully, and remember any particular *Theme mood* which may have characterized your dream; the message it gives could be very useful in your life.

If a person known to you has taken on the trappings of a king

Only the dreamer can interpret his or her own dream successfully. If you dream that someone has become a king-like figure, this is how you are seeing them in waking life. A father figure, perhaps; or an unapproachable 'king of the castle'. It may be mere infatuation, but it could be that this person really does have something very important for your life and happiness.

See also: HERO; WISE PERSON

KITE

If you or someone else is flying a kite in your dream, it implies that something rather insubstantial is being kept aloft: an enterprise, perhaps, that is liable to collapse if there is a slight change of circumstances. The nature of the wind, like public opinion, is somewhat fickle, and the support your enterprise is receiving might suddenly disappear.

See also: GLIDER

L

LABYRINTH

Any dream situation where you find yourself in some kind of labyrinth or maze, implies that you are not 'lost'; you probably know where you are and where you want to go, but have arrived at a 'Catch-22' situation with frustrations at every turn. In the family, at work, in society, it happens sometimes that whatever you try to do is likely to increase your problems, and your *Inner feelings* see this situation as a virtual labyrinth. It may be a small problem, or it may encompass your whole life. If the dream itself offers no clues as to the best way forward, at least it is telling you to take an objective view of your difficulties.

See also: LOST

LADDER

The whole point of a ladder is to enable you to climb to a higher place, and in dreams this higher place is probably within your own mind. The *Self* is often symbolised in dreams as a building. You normally live on the ground floor; your *Personal unconscious mind* is downstairs in the basement; upstairs are your rarely visited higher intuitive faculties, or your intelligence when you really concentrate on some problem. If you very rarely visit the upper floor, there may be no stairs in your dream house, and this is where a ladder comes in useful. It is a means of escape from your own limitations. If you have been given the chance to explore the higher regions of your psyche, do not fail to take advantage of the situation.

See also: CLIMBING; ESCAPING

LAKE   *or pond: enclosed water*

Your dream lake may be dark and mysterious, or it may be sunlit and bright, depending perhaps on your own mood. Unless you have reason to dream of a real lake relating to your past experiences, this dream lake is probably an allegorical picture of your own self. Its depths represent your *Personal unconscious mind*, and anything in, on or around it, particularly if they appear to be living creatures, are likely to represent your own thoughts, feelings, ideas and impressions. The surface of the lake will represent your emotions, and these may be placid or disturbed. Perhaps you have had cause recently to think and feel very deeply about your life; if the water is muddy, perhaps you have been feeling guilty or uncertain as to the way ahead. These ideas need to be linked to any other features in the dream.

See also: DAM; SEA; WATER

LAMENESS

In dreams your feet represent your own journey through the world, as seen by the inner self. If you dream you have become lame, then plainly something is impeding your smooth progress. As always, there are at least two ways of looking at this: it could be your everyday, practical progress through life, and the lameness in your dream could be real, physical problems which trouble you, though they should have no effect on your dream life. More likely, it could be referring to your spiritual or psychological progress from day to day. There may have been recent *Trigger events* which gave rise to the symbol. These could involve a touch of envy, if others seem to be travelling through life and gaining success apparently effortlessly while you flounder. The same applies if someone else in your dream is showing lameness. They could be envying you in some respect. A feeling of patience in real life is required.

See also: FEET; JOURNEY

Laughter   (A theme mood)

Laughter often features in *Children's dreams*, but is rarely to be experienced as an adult. There seems to be something rather unpleasant about dream laughter, as it is usually directed against someone – very likely yourself, and is reflecting the fact that you feel you have made a fool of yourself in some way. The purpose of dreaming is to instruct rather than to entertain, and you need to study the contents of such a dream very conscientiously.

See also: Amusement

LAUNDRY

Dream clothes represent the personality and individual characteristics. Dirt connected with clothes implies faults and less-than-pleasant features associated with the people who wear them. A dream laundry represents a state of affairs that is intended to remove those stains, or actions that are intended to 'turn over a new leaf'. Soiled sheets carry a strong implication of guilt connected with bed and the bedroom. General dirt on household items, and furniture which is being cleaned implies that a person – either the dreamer or someone known to them personally – has been neglectful in some way, or their living conditions have been neglected to a disturbing degree.

See also: CLOTHES; DIRT

LIBRARY

Dream books normally represent knowledge or wisdom, unless they are plainly antique and valuable in their own right. A collection of books represents a source of knowledge which the dreamer relies upon. An individual book can symbolise a lifestyle, in the manner of a biography: changing your library book in a dream suggests that you are about to change your lifestyle in some important way. Over and above these meanings, interpreting a dream about books depends very much on what books mean to the dreamer personally. To one they may symbolise romance; to another adventure; to yet another academic study; and visiting a dream library may forecast an upturn in these activities.

See also: BOOKS

LILIES

Rather a specialized flower as a dream symbol: purity, virginity, death and funerals are frequently associated with them, and they may well represent any of these events or qualities. In an example dream (see *Dream diagrams*) the dreamer buys a bunch of lilies to symbolise that he was accepting the inevitability of death. Water lilies fill a different role: they may be used as a symbol of yogic meditation. Floating on the surface of water they can symbolise the innocent, unsuspecting, conscious self, but this naive self is blissfully unaware of the dark depths of the *Personal unconscious mind*, possibly with the sinister *Shadow* of repressed contents, lurking beneath its conscious self-awareness..

See also: FLOWER; FUNERAL; LAKE; WATER

LOST

It is a common experience to dream that you have become lost. The nature of having 'lost direction' depends on what 'direction' you consider paramount in your life. It may be an everyday case of having run up against problems in your professional or family life, or it may be much deeper than that: it may be referring to your spiritual progress through life, or having 'gone astray' in the religious sense. It sometimes happens that you dream of places familiar to you as a child, and think about going home, only to remember that you no longer live there. This dream symbol could be drawing your attention to the fact that there is more to life than the mere material aspects of physical existence; in this case you need to search for a spiritual dimension which will enable you to find the right direction in your waking life.

See also: LABYRINTH; UNEMPLOYED

THE KEY TO DREAM ANALYSIS

Love (A theme mood)

There are of course different kinds of 'love', and different ways of feeling it: there is sexual lust which could be called 'love'; there is family love such as a mother might feel for her child; and there is spiritual love which overrides personal feelings. Any powerful feeling during a dream or which lingers after waking, drops an equally powerful hint as to the nature and purpose of the dream, and only the dreamer personally is really able to interpret it.

Lucid dreams

It sometimes happens that you become aware that you are asleep and dreaming, and this is known as a 'lucid dream'. You will then discover that you are able to control the events in your dream, making the dream characters do what you want them to do, and even allow yourself to travel around at will. Some dream books recommend encouraging this faculty in yourself and making a habit of it, resulting in a certain boost in self-confidence and a strengthening of the ego. But this dream book warns against the practice. The ultimate aim of our dreams and the dreaming process is to clear out the dark contents of the *Personal unconscious mind* before it becomes too heavy a spiritual burden, and this is a function of the *Inner feelings*. The everyday ego cannot assist in the process, much as it would like to. When you experience a lucid dream, use it to your own advantage: to be forewarned is to be forearmed; you will still be asleep, but conscious of what is happening. Allow the dream events to unfold without interference, go along with it like a character in a play, and you may be amazed at what you will learn.

LUGGAGE *baggage, burdens which you feel you need to carry*

In the dream world all life is a journey, and the baggage you carry with you comprises everything that has been acquired by your personality: loves and hates, hopes and fears, passions and desires, habits, customs, religious practices and beliefs, prejudices and preconceptions. Some people have acquired so much baggage that they can hardly move; others travel light. If you dream that your own luggage is too heavy and burdensome, the time has come to lighten the load. You can do this by finding time to quieten your thoughts and emotions, and let go of all unnecessary trappings. If you normally feel passionate about various aspects of life, remember that the only passions important to your life are the passions of faith (as opposed to 'belief'), patience, and sincerity.

See also:　　OBSTACLES

M

MACHINERY *Mechanical devices*

Anything of this nature in your dream is sure to represent some aspect of materiality, the workings of civilisation, industry, manufacturing, and impersonal progress. You may be looking at these machines with a feeling of apprehension, wondering whether you can cope with their complicated controls. This is a fairly common situation when you are approaching some new situation in waking life, a new job, perhaps, when you are not sure whether you will fit in. Another possibility is that you are looking with interest and want to become involved: perhaps you have been feeling left out of things. Or again the sight of machinery may repel you, and you want to escape from it and seek something more personal and peaceful: your own true self, perhaps!

See also: FACTORY

MANDALA

The 'magic circle' of a mandala derives from the Sanskrit, an ancient concept expressing the universal principle of the *Self*. The following section on *Mandala diagrams* shows how the circle (representing a globe) very tellingly describes the process of dreaming, and the relationship between the conscious and unconscious minds. In dreams, a first realization of the self as a spiritual principle will give rise to images reflecting this with regard to the dreamer's own normal everyday experiences. The self is not something new or alien, but the whole person, both inwardly and outwardly, and dreams depicting this will often feature a circle, or a square, or a combination of the two: a town square with flowers and trees; a group of dancers advancing and retreating to form a symmetrical pattern; an ancient stone circle; a flower with radiating petals. Images such as these may mark the commencement of a truly spiritual phase of your own life.

See also: CLOCK; FLOWER

THE KEY TO DREAM ANALYSIS

Mandala diagrams illustrating the dreaming process

The *Self* can be visualized as a globe and pictured as a circle, like the earth itself, with the upper half representing the conscious waking mind bathed in light, the lower half representing the unconscious sleeping mind shrouded in darkness. The horizon represents the division between day and night, waking and sleeping, conscious and unconscious. All the worrying thoughts and impressions of the day – or the period when we are awake – tend to be pushed down into the unconscious mind where they are worked upon by the hidden *Inner feelings*, and finally processed into a new perspective composed of symbolic truths, to be re-presented to the conscious mind in the form of dreams. Below the inner feelings lurks the *Shadow*, the unaccepted and disowned matters which have passed through the thoughts and feelings – matters perhaps too unpleasant to be processed by the inner feelings into an acceptable form.

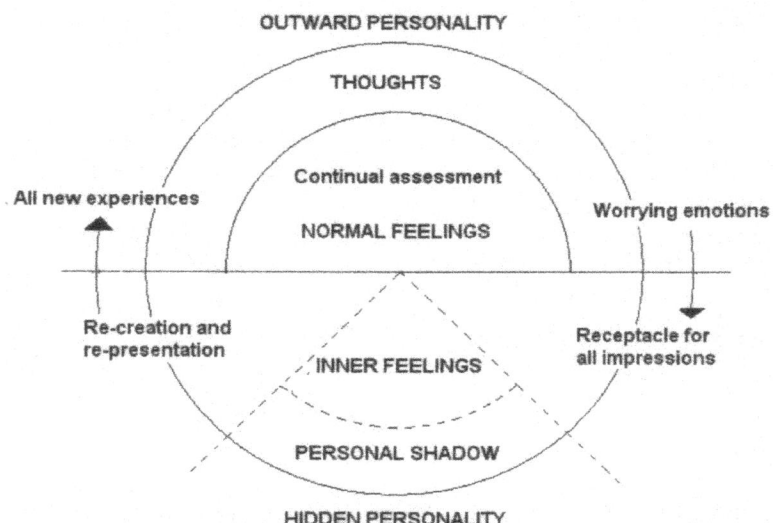

THE KEY TO DREAM ANALYSIS

All the mental and emotional impressions of the day are pushed into the unconscious mind in a disorganized, confused jumble. This is why *Evening dreams* if we wake soon after going to sleep, or *Dozing dreams* when we snap out of it after dropping off for a moment in our armchair, will seldom make sense when we try to analyse them. During the sleeping period as they are worked upon by the inner feelings they begin to take on a more organized form until they reach their most meaningful structure towards dawn. Dreams may emerge at any time, but Dawn dreams are always the most vivid and memorable.

The background nature of dreams tends to vary in a very subtle way throughout the sleeping period, and in order to appreciate this it is really necessary to study the concept of the *World dream*. There is an old adage which says: 'as above, so below', and in this sense the world is the macrocosm, humans the microcosm. The world mandala (overleaf) expresses the concept of Gaia, the world seen as a self-supporting entity. Here again the horizon represents the difference between night and day: in this case the spiritual day of superhuman principles above the horizon, and below it the world of nature – in spiritual darkness. As in the mandala diagrams above, it is to be seen as a cycle, with dawn (and human birth) on the left, sunset on the right. The beginning of the 'world dream' is the raw material: solid rock, earth and minerals. In mythological terms the Archangel Lucifer fell to earth in a blaze of light to rule over the dark world of materiality. At first there is chaos and a jumble of rocks and earth. Now as the dream progresses plants appear and struggle to establish themselves. Then animals appear, feeding on the plants and on each other, gradually developing increasing mental and emotional powers. Finally humans appear, primitive at first, until when dawn breaks they become bathed in the light of the spiritual forces above them. The *Dawn dreams* of the earth itself should correspond with the perfection of the human psyche.

The spiritual status of humans is normally fated to sink from birth onwards, passing through the human level during babyhood, through the animal level as a pre-teen child, through the plant level as a teenager, finally to reach the material level in adulthood. To follow the subtle movement of the world dream is to reverse this course, one's psychic level then passing from the material, through the plant and the animals levels, finally to reach the point of human rebirth and beyond.

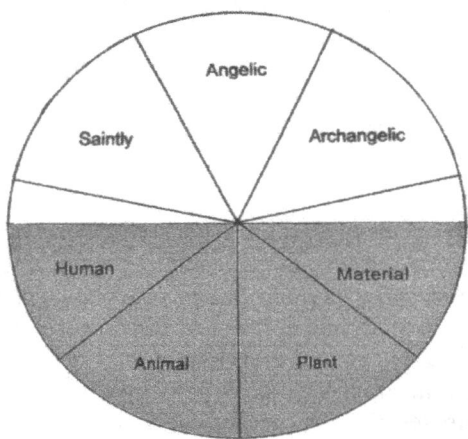

THE KEY TO DREAM ANALYSIS

If we superimpose the dream mandala onto the world mandala we can see that the progressive nature of the development of our dreams corresponds with the 'world dream' from a chaotic state, with a jumble of materialistic images, through the plant nature, the animal nature, finally to reach the human nature towards the end of the sleeping period. Plants are obliged, albeit unconsciously, to struggle for their existence, competing with other plants which would smother them. Animals are moral creatures, in the sense that they behave according to their own rules, but they too can be aggressive in fixing their own boundaries and establishing supremacy. It follows that our dreams during this corresponding period of sleep tend to be of an adversarial nature.

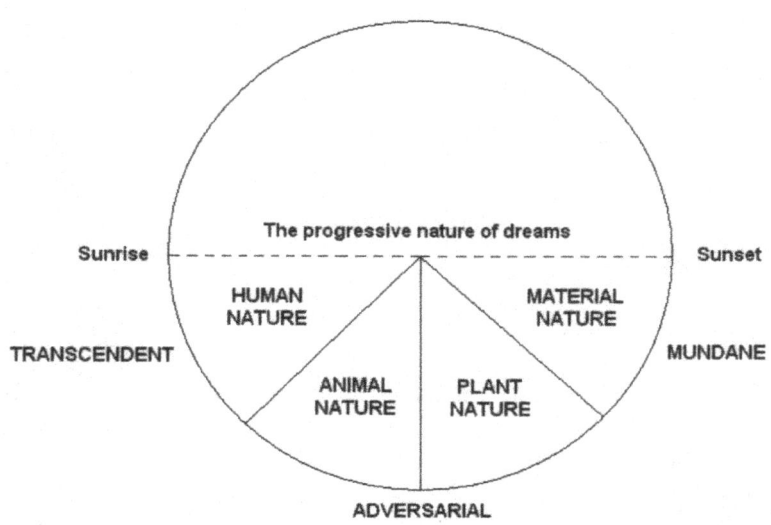

To take the matter further, suppose we have been worried about something, and have taken our worried thoughts to bed with us. We know our inner feelings are able to offer solutions to many of our problems, which they project by way of dreams. But when this happens we can observe that the nature of these solutions will vary according to the length of time we have been asleep before waking – according in fact to the transient nature of the underlying world dream.

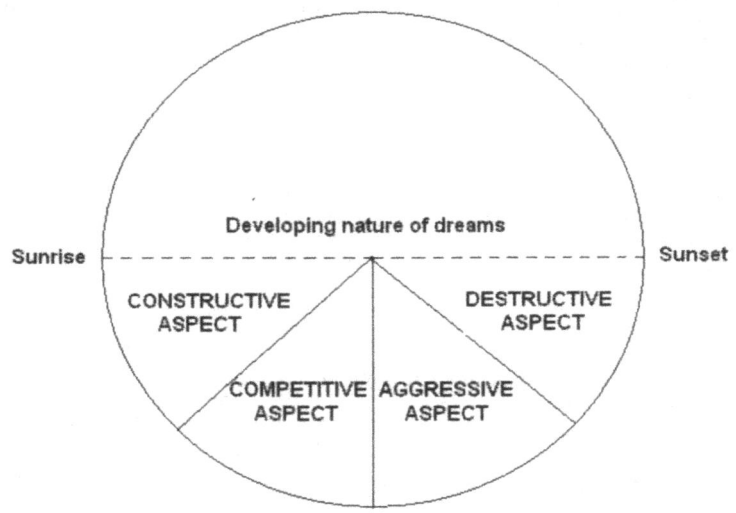

If we refer to *Freudian dreams*, *Adlerian dreams*, and *Jungian dreams* and apply their principles to a dream mandala, we will see that they correspond in a striking manner. Ordinary everyday dreams are concerned with material problems, material benefits, material advancement. Adler raised the question of 'power-seeking', which is allied to plant life striving to gain a root-hold on the earth. Freud concerned himself with sexual instincts with the accent on morality. Jung was more interested in higher human possibilities which aim for the same goal as the world dream itself: the perfection of the human psyche.

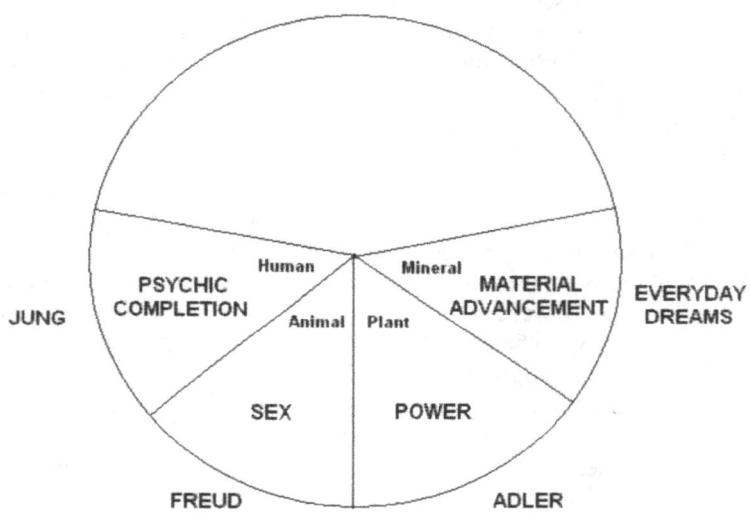

MARKET *or any busy, bustling place*

The dream market represents yourself meeting with the rest of society, interacting with people in the way normal to you. The symbol by itself expresses your attitude to others, and if it was merely an incident in a narrative dream, any *Theme mood* associated with it will be important. Some people need to mix and socialize more than they do; others need to cut down on social interaction. We all need to withdraw from society at times and spend a quiet time alone.

See also: CARNIVAL; PLAYING

Meditation   *(affecting your dream life)*

'A quiet time alone' is echoed in this category, and of course different people may have very different ideas about the meaning of 'meditation'. There are two basic possibilities here, which are diametrically opposed to one another, and they concern one's attitude to higher matters, or spiritual possibilities. If your 'meditation' is simply aimed at finding the best course of action in some sphere or another, this is 'pondering' rather than 'meditating'. Religious or yogic meditation may be directed towards keeping out unwanted influences, or 'rising above them'. But the whole *Self* includes all influences, good and bad. A healthy dream life depends on the free circulation of influences within the self, and 'bad' influences should have no ill effect. Suppose someone succeeds in shutting out bad influences through religious meditation, the chances are they will have shut out good influences as well, because of course we cannot know whether something is going to be good or bad before we have become aware of it. Some kinds of religious imagery picture the meditating self as a pure lotus flower floating on calm waters. This may be an attractive image, but taken too far the practice can cut off contact with everything beneath the surface of the water – representing the *Personal unconscious mind*. When this happens the *Inner feelings* will be unable to function in any meaningful way. Any dreams you then experience will be ego-dreams leading you nowhere. The only kind of meditation that will help your dream life along (and set you on a course compatible with the flow of the *World dream* aimed towards human psychic completion), is purely passive: allowing your thoughts and emotions to subside, in full awareness, thereby laying yourself open to such influences as may arise from a source higher than the spiritual level of ordinary humans. On a note of caution: anything approaching a state of trance should be strictly avoided, as it will result in an unwanted and quite unnecessary invasion of influences from a source *lower* than the proper human level.

MIST *the way ahead obscured*

Not quite as baffling as a *Fog*, but you still cannot see the way ahead clearly. The dream image is probably reflecting a state of affairs that has arisen in your waking life, when old certainties have turned into doubts. Patience is called for, and this is not a time for snap decisions. In due course a new direction and a better set of circumstances will present themselves as mist seldom lasts long. Wait until the way ahead is quite clear before making important decisions.

MONSTER

Something very frightening and quite unexpected has suddenly come to life. The chances are it has emerged from your own *Personal unconscious mind*, a part of your own *Shadow*, a set of characteristics you thought forgotten, a dark idea you thought safely in the past. A dream *Crocodile*, or alligator, or an unknown horror has emerged from the swamp and is seriously threatening your safety. It may be connected with someone else, a family member perhaps, who is behaving in a startling manner. If someone you know seems to have turned into a monster in your dream, it could be a very serious warning of psychological problems on the part of the person concerned. It sometimes happens that a bout of mental instability or insanity is heralded within the family by this dream image.

See also: ADVERSARY; DEMON; DRAGON; *Nightmares*

MONUMENT   *a memorial built to impress*

A monument implies the wish that something or somebody should not be forgotten by posterity. This is the case with a war memorial, for instance, or an impressive tombstone, or a statue set on a tall pillar. These things are not created purely to impress people with the importance of whatever they are meant to commemorate: they are powerful statements of strongly-felt emotion. In effect they are trying to turn emotions into something solid. Emotions provide the key to the dream significance of this symbol. Something has affected the dreamer very deeply, something perhaps that he or she does not want to put into words, but which has taken on almost tangible solidity.

See also: IDOL; STATUE

MOON

One of the most ancient of dream symbols, along with sun, dawn, and night. Its meaning depends rather upon your own cultural background. In some cultures the moon is the great time-keeper; to others merely a comforting light in the dark. But to both it has a powerful emotional appeal, and may actually affect the human body in the way its gravity draws moisture towards itself: it certainly has a powerful effect upon the tides of the ocean. To the dreamer it implies emotional reassurance.

See also: SUN

Morality

The *Inner feelings* are the seat of conscience, and questions of morality when they occur in dreams usually relate to matters of conscience and feelings of guilt which need to be worked through. Even small matters which may be not quite honest are of concern to the inner feelings, matters which the outer feelings or everyday emotions would think unimportant and happily forget. The study of dreams tells us that such things form part of the *Shadow* if they are not accepted and resolved, and add to the burden of the *Personal unconscious mind* in a way which may seem out of all proportion to the importance of some seemingly insignificant act. As far as the inner feelings are concerned, the concept of 'guilt' involves acts which have affected other people in a negative way, hurting someone's feelings perhaps, diminishing them to some extent. This is because all people are linked on the level of the inner feelings. Whilst people still live in the soul-level of materiality these things may have no significance. But once an individual begins to take the 'return journey', to go with the flow of the *World dream* and follow the course of evolution, such things become increasingly important.

MOUNTAIN

If the mountain is a barrier or a threat

It may be a mountain range, or a cliff face, in effect forming a very high wall which is hemming you in and impeding your progress, possibly even threatening to fall on you and crush you. It is really a very clear symbol of some real-life circumstance which is having a similar effect: a material or even a psychological situation which is going to cause you problems.

THE KEY TO DREAM ANALYSIS

If you are climbing the mountain

You may be 'scaling the heights of ambition', or hoping to do just that, or the dream mountain to be climbed may symbolise problems that you need to overcome, difficulties at work, or marital or family problems. You may be in danger of sliding back down the mountain, and this quite a common dream experience, or you may have passed the peak and seem to be on the way down. Ice and snow on the top of the mountain implies that you are going through hard times which will soon improve as you travel beyond the peak.. Sometimes the dreamer feels very strongly that the dream mountain has some sort of spiritual quality, and this is not really a very good omen. It implies that he or she is trying to take conscious control of matters which are better left to a more submissive attitude of 'what will be, will be'. There should be no doubt in the dreamer's mind concerning the identity of this mountain in real life.

See also: CLIMBING

MUD

In dream symbolism, earth or soil represents solid materiality – the indisputable nature of facts as they really are. Water represents the emotions, and often the sexual desires. If there is mud along your path, the significance is that your way through life is being hampered by an excess of these feelings on your part. Sometimes a dream may picture you struggling through mud *alongside* a path or roadway. In this case the implication is that you are in some way following your own desires to an extent which is alarming even you, and you have become aware that you need to stop floundering and regain the hard road. Quite commonly a dream may have you driving or walking down an increasingly muddy track; you may even be in danger of becoming stuck permanently. The chances are that the meaning of dreams such as this will be perfectly obvious to you. Passions and desires can readily become a sticking point.

See also: DIRT; WATER

THE KEY TO DREAM ANALYSIS

MUSEUM   *A display of old relics*

A museum display represents things and ideas that seem to you to be no longer of use, though they may once have been admired. In a real-life museum visitors are expected to be quiet and respectful, almost reverent in the presence of values once held dear but now long gone. Is this the atmosphere of your dream? It may be that the dreamer is behaving badly in a museum, scoffing at the exhibits and upsetting the other visitors. In real life it is usually people and institutions with old-fashioned values that are symbolised by a dream museum, and the dreamer may be respectful in their presence, or scornful. What may seem to you a useless antique may still be of value to someone else: it could be that you are hurting someone's feelings in waking life.

See also: ANTIQUE; MORALITY

Mythmaking dreams

Ancient myths were rarely sheer flights of fancy. Their stories reflected the descent of mankind from childlike beginnings to the sophistication of a civilized way of life. A study of the *World dream* will show very clearly the spiritual background to this descent, symbolising original human instincts becoming adulterated by the acquisition of instincts more appropriate to animals and plants. These things came to the awareness of sensitive people by way of dreams and visions. *Children's dreams* often show the same characteristics today. Different races of mankind have produced differing myths reflecting the descent of their race from their own 'Garden of Eden'. The process may be the same, but the imagery will be quite different. There is no 'correct' way of looking at these things because they do not have a material or scientific base. Adults of any race nowadays are highly unlikely to experience anything approaching the mythmaking dreams of old.

N

NAKED

Nakedness in a dream is portraying the person without the trappings of personality, the social veneer, the acquired habits and characteristics. Some people habitually see themselves as naked and unashamed during their dreams, because the *Inner feelings* are showing them how they really are without any pretence. Inhibitions belong to the outer feelings; the inner feelings have no inhibitions. If you dream you are naked and feel the need to hide your nakedness, this means that in waking life you have been made to drop your social disguises against your will. People have seen through the social disguise of your *Persona* and you are finding this an embarrassment.

See also: CLOTHES

Nightmares

The original meaning of a nightmare, also known as a night-hag, or 'the riding of the witch', was not simply a bad dream. It described a physical sensation as though a weight had been placed on the chest, resulting in the feeling of being crushed. This is most likely to be a medical problem, caused by a condition usually called 'apnoea' when breathing ceases to be automatic and stops long enough to cause a lack of oxygenated blood to the heart – in effect a minor heart attack. It may or may not be accompanied by an actual bad dream. More usually the term 'nightmare' is used simply to describe a terrifying dream, which may have been triggered by some real-life event. Children especially are sometimes apt to experience the 'night terrors' when they are liable to scream and thrash about while still asleep, though they may have no later recollection of any accompanying dream. The majority of bad dreams however arise from the normal cycling process of the dreaming self, involving a frightening apparition belonging to the *Shadow*, and consisting of unresolved problems which have become lodged in the *Personal unconscious mind*.

Non-self dreams

A term used for any dream in which the dreamer finds that he or she is someone else: dreaming on behalf of someone else; experiencing someone else's problems and traumatic incidents in the form of so-called *Veridical dreams*; or sometimes experiencing an incident in the life of an animal. Some such dreams could be said to involve personal intuitive contact, but perhaps the majority involve complete strangers. So-called *Reincarnation dreams* sometimes involve long-dead people. It should be remembered that the *Inner feelings* which are normally responsible for assembling dream images, also have open contact with the inner feelings of other people, and on a non-material plane neither space nor time are necessarily barriers to shared images. It is not a subject that lends itself well to psychological theory, but practical experience will show that such *Intuitive dreams* are very real and by no means infrequent.

O

OBSTACLES *barriers to progress*

Dream obstacles can take almost any form, but they all reflect real-life obstacles to the dreamer's smooth progress through life. They may be solidly material obstacles in the dream, but in waking life these obstacles are more likely to be purely psychological or social. The dream details need searching carefully for clues as to the real nature of these impediments. Quite often someone may dream that he or she is being pursued, but cannot make progress for whatever reason. The case is similar, and interpretation will depend on the symbolic handicap that is holding the dreamer back.

See also: CHASING; LUGGAGE

Oedipus dreams

Sigmund Freud was a pioneer in the field of dream analysis, and ascribed paramount importance to the repressed sexual content of dreams. Named after the mythological figure who unwittingly killed his father and married his mother, an Oedipus complex characterises a boy or young man who possesses a (usually unconscious) sexual desire for his mother, and a feeling of jealousy or hatred directed at his father. Dreams may indicate these characteristics in a disguised form, amended perhaps by what Freud termed the *Endo-psychic censor*. Freud also coined the phrase 'Electra complex' to describe a parallel situation applying to girls.

OPPONENT

Your dream opponent may of course be an actual person with whom you have problems, and the dream should be totally straightforward. But if this is not the case, the type of opponent needs narrowing down and identifying: there are at least two alternative possibilities. The *Adversary* is an opponent who has emerged from your own *Personal unconscious mind*, an enigmatic figure composed perhaps of personal characteristics which trouble you but which you are not prepared to deal with in waking life. The *Assailant* is a figure composed of factors from outside of yourself which have become symbolized as an individual opponent. The dream itself should offer clues to enable you to identify this threatening figure, and then perhaps you will be able to deal with it.

See also: Frightening dreams

P

Painful duty   (A theme mood)

You may awake from a dream with the feeling of having done your duty, however unpleasant, a feeling uncomfortably close to self righteousness. Your *Inner feelings* could be dropping you the hint that you are becoming too involved in the concept of morality and losing sight of the all-important qualities of empathy, sympathy and compassion. The inner feelings themselves are concerned with morality in the sense of avoiding guilt, particularly in avoiding causing harm or discomfort to others, because all people are psychically linked on the level of these inner feelings – also known as the higher emotional centre. What they *can* be critical of by way of dreams is the sort of 'man-made morality' that can *cause* harm and discomfort to others quite unnecessarily. Whatever the dream involved, the feeling of 'painful duty' is suspect and the dream details need to be analysed with this in mind.

PAINTING

Applying covering coats of paint

Plainly something is being covered up and made to look different, possibly more attractive than it was before. Who is doing the painting in the dream, and what is being disguised? These are the crucial questions, and when these details have been established there should be no doubt about the meaning of the dream.

Painting a picture

An artistic creation: whether the subject is abstract, a scene, an event, a person, something is being portrayed that was not visible before. Again, who is doing the painting? Something is being shown in a new light, or attention is being drawn to something that previously went unrecognised; perhaps something is being falsified, or exaggerated. Only the dreamer personally can decipher the cryptic content of the dream.

See also: ART

Paralysis in sleep

This can be a frightening phenomenon – a state possibly half way between sleeping and waking when you want to wake fully but cannot move, involving a totally helpless feeling of being paralysed. This sensation is sometimes linked to *Lucid dreams* in which you become aware that you are dreaming. During most lucid dreams the dreamer is able to manipulate the dream characters and events, but sleep paralysis prevents this happening. The physical body perhaps has become 'out of sync', remaining asleep while the mind has awoken. If it could be called a dream, sleep paralysis seems to be expressing the wish to alter physical characteristics which cannot be altered in practice. When it occurs in the course of a dream, it certainly implies helplessness to act without first allowing the dream events to be completed. This can sometimes be linked to an unpleasant real-life situation which must be allowed to run its course before finding a solution at which the dream itself may hint.

See also: Nightmares

PARROT

Parrots are acclaimed for their mimicry and are traditionally taught words and phrases, although obviously they will not understand what they are saying. This is the meaning of 'parrot' as a symbol. A schoolchild may 'parrot' words without having taken in their true significance, and a younger child just learning to speak may also copy sounds before learning their meaning: this is part of the natural learning process, and probably the best way even for adults to learn a foreign language. To dream that a parrot sits on your or someone else's shoulder does not necessarily mean that you or they don't know what you're talking about. A dream of this nature therefore is quite likely to happen when you are struggling to learn a foreign language; as often as not a parrot will be sitting on your shoulder!

See also: BIRDS

PATH   *A way along which you walk*

This must be one of the most ancient of dream symbols, representing the dreamer's own way through life. In modern times, driving a car will have much the same meaning, describing your normal daily progress and the difficulties and obstacles you may meet along the way. By itself, the dream symbol is no more than that – the fact or background of your own life. The factors to be met with along the path: the ease or difficulty with which you make progress, the nature of the surface, perhaps muddy, rough, rock-strewn, or covered with snow and ice; the people and things you encounter along the path, the scenery through which you walk – all these things will need analysing separately to form a picture of your own progress through life.

See also: CAR; DRIVING; FEET; JOURNEY; ROAD

PEARL

Actual pearls of course are produced by oysters, within their hard shell, and deep below the sea. Symbolically, a 'pearl of great price' is a non-material treasure hidden deep within the innermost emotions, beneath the sea of the unconscious mind. Even the mere awareness of such things is to be treasured: to complete the cycling process of the *Personal unconscious mind* and bring light to the darkest parts of the self may not be fully attainable, but to make progress in this direction is certainly a personal 'pearl' of inestimable value.

See also: *Collective unconscious; Cycle of the dreaming self;* GOLD; JEWELS; TREASURE

Persona

The early psychoanalysts likened the persona to a mask or public disguise which the person habitually wears. This is an area of the psyche sometimes appearing as a separate dream figure, or one of the *Archetypes of the unconscious mind*, portraying the dreamer as he or she normally present themselves to others, or the way in which they would like others to think of them. In the case of some people the persona is a powerful character; in others less so.

Personal dreams

Occasionally, dreams plainly relate to others rather than the dreamer personally, and may be *Intuitive dreams* experiencing incidents in the lives of others, or even *Reincarnation dreams* when the other person featured is long dead. Dreams such as this can be interpreted by people other than the dreamer personally, who has merely acted as a receiver or recorder of someone else's traumatic experiences. The great majority of dreams however are personal in content, referring to events in the dreamer's life and their own psychic contents. A personal dream, therefore, is one which can only be fully understood or interpreted by the dreamer personally, although others may analyse the details of what Freud would have called its 'manifest contents'.

See also: *Impersonal dreams*

Personal unconscious mind

Early psychoanalysts expounded the existence of the unconscious mind, and if you refer to the section on *Dream diagrams* you will see how the personal unconscious works in a continually cycling movement, the conscious thoughts and impressions of the waking day sinking down into the dark world of the unconscious mind, where they are received and worked over by the hidden *Inner feelings*, to be pushed back into awareness in the form of dreams and visions, waking thoughts and sudden inspirations, or if these things are too unpleasant to be contemplated, they may be drawn down as though by gravity into the deepest and darkest part of the personal unconscious, where they remain in the form of the *Shadow*. In simplified form, the personal unconscious mind can be given the general term of 'the subconscious', a term which seems to lessen its undoubted importance and significance in the case of any individual who hopes to work towards the perfection of the human psyche.

PIG

As a symbol the pig has a variable significance depending upon the race, the religion or the cultural background of the person concerned. Because it was foremost on the list of proscribed animals as presented by Moses, within those religions that follow Moses to this day it can be perceived as something to be shunned. People of other cultures were taught that the words which come out of one's mouth can be far more damaging to one's spiritual status than the food which goes in, and for them the pig lost its unclean status. To many people the pig has always represented a major part of their staple diet, and is thought of in familiar terms. As a domesticated animal both greedy and intelligent, as a wild boar fierce and untamed, or as a pink and naked piglet symbolic perhaps of sexual peccadilloes, there are many types of people who can be symbolised by a pig in dreams.

See also: ANIMALS

PIT   *Any unidentified hole in the ground*

Like the *Abyss*, this is one of the most basic of dream symbols, representing the *Personal unconscious mind*. Matters which have not been fully dealt with by the conscious mind pass down into the dark recesses of the unconscious. As a dream symbol it may warn against the un-wisdom of throwing unwanted objects into the pit, hoping to see the last of them, because they will not simply disappear. If they are not matters which can be dealt with by the *Inner feelings* and re-presented to the conscious mind in the form of dreams, they are liable to form part of the mysterious *Shadow* that lurks in the lowest, darkest part of the psyche. A dream pit may be warning or gently reminding you of the need to deal with matters thoroughly as they arise, and not hope that unpleasant facts will go away by simply ignoring them. If your dream involves falling into, or pushing somebody into the pit, or being pushed into it, refer to the entry under *Abyss* for further details. The symbolism will be the same in both cases.

See also: CELLAR; *Yin and yang*

THE KEY TO DREAM ANALYSIS

Pity (A theme mood)

This is not a very pleasant feeling; it is rather too close to 'contempt', and implies a feeling of superiority over whoever may be the subject of the dream. Arrogance is something we should all strive to avoid, and nobody likes to feel 'pitied'. When this feeling colours your dream, you need to take very careful stock of all the dream details. Who or what is being pitied? If it is a real person known to you, a little self-criticism is called for. If you are pitying an apparent stranger, could this be you? Study the *Archetypes of the unconscious mind* and decide if you are trying to reject, or belittle, or criticise your own intuitive capacity, which is warning you against some conscious decision which you have recently made.

Plant-nature dreams

A brief study of the *World dream* will show the universal background to our dream life. Ordinary, everyday dreams of relationships, events and places correspond with the material section of the world dream, the earth, rocks and minerals. When somebody has been striving to break away from some material situation, seeking a new dimension, perhaps involving some sort of power, particularly if they have been feeling aggression, or suffering from the hostility or bullying of others, his or her dreams will tend to correspond with the plant section of nature.

See also: Adlerian dreams

PLAYING

If you are watching without taking part

Whatever the nature of the game, others are presumably enjoying the activity and you, the dreamer, are on the fringe. The question is, do you want to join in or not, and if not, why are you standing watching? The game may be symbolising the rat-race of life from which you have thankfully retired; or you may have been feeling shut out from the social and business scene and feel that you would like nothing better than to be admitted. In this case, it may have been no more than a *Wish fulfilment dream.* The symbolism is clear enough, but what are your feelings on the matter?

If you are taking part in the game

Again, the game is likely to symbolise the hurly-burly of life, and it is your own attitude towards the game and the other players that will hold the significance of the dream. The *Theme mood* or emotions which you felt on waking and recalling the dream will give you the clue. Did you enjoy taking part, or would you prefer to walk away and leave them to it?

See also: BALL; CARNIVAL; MARKET; PROCESSION

PLOUGHING *Carving a furrow in the ground*

Earth represents materiality, the potential from which you can create the wherewithal of life, build a business empire, rear a family. If you are a farmer, ploughing can represent next year's income and your future welfare. It is an age-old symbol, of course, and a well-ploughed field is a sign of satisfaction and security. If things go wrong during the process, the symbols involved will have significance for the future.

See also: DESERT; DIGGING; EARTH MOTHER

POLICE

Out-and-out criminals may have a different perception; but for the majority of people a policeman represents a principle for the good. Most people care about their own characters, and would prefer others to see them as basically good rather than bad, and a dream policeman in their case will represent a guardian of good conduct. If you have feelings of guilt about anything at all, a dream policeman may be watching you suspiciously. To follow unspoken rules of conduct through life is not the same as excessive morality or 'do-gooding': it is to achieve and maintain a fair balance in your own psyche. Your *Inner feelings*, as your own seat of conscience, are interested in all your actions and thoughts for this purpose. All people are psychically linked on that deep level, and to hurt another in any way is the same as hurting yourself: this is why no-one can escape the consequences of his or her actions in the long run. As a basic *Archetype,* the symbolic policeman is watching you! To dream you are carrying a friendly policeman in your *Car* implies that you have made or are about to make a morally correct decision.

See also: MORALITY; UNIFORM

PRECIPICE   *A steep drop down*

There are numerous symbols of the unconscious mind, the edge of awareness over which all your unwanted and half-forgotten ideas fall out of sight – but not out of mind. But this stark symbol may be more practical: if the track you are following ends on the edge of a cliff, the warning could scarcely be clearer: there will be problems ahead if you continue on your present course. In either case the symbol is a warning to the dreamer, whether in physical or in psychological terms: take careful stock of where you are heading, change course, and look before you leap.

See also: ABYSS; PIT

Predictive dreams

Some dream books recommend trying to induce predictive dreams by concentrating on some issue, or perhaps on potential newspaper headlines in the hope of dreaming about events to come. But *this* dream book warns against it. If you are going to dream of future events, a much higher source of intelligence than your everyday brains will decide it for you. If you succeed in doing it yourself, you will have short-circuited or disrupted the dreaming process by forcing your own ego into territory where it has no business to go. Genuine predictive dreams usually tell of events that will take place within a few days, and almost always they are personal matters which will affect the dreamer alone. They warn of events that will take place, so that the dreamer is prepared for them when they arrive. They may also impart information about the lives of others, and when they do the matter should usually be kept private. Some dreams may seem to be predicting events, when analysis will show that the prediction is symbolic and allegorical, and not to be taken literally.

PROCESSION

If you are taking part in the dream procession

Were you happy to be following the crowd during the dream? The symbol is rather suspect: you are being swept along by what seems to be the majority view; individuals in a procession do not decide where they are going, or how fast, and they are not in a position to change their minds. It might be better for you to hold back and rethink your own position. Majority decisions tend to echo the lowest and narrowest rather than the highest or broadest of viewpoints.

If you are watching the procession without taking part

The symbol of a procession seems to be expressing the popular view, and the fact that you are watching with interest without joining in implies that you want to remain independent. You may or may not agree with the popular cause; the nature of the procession, the people taking part and the other symbols involved, should explain the dream.

See also: CARNIVAL

Purifying dreams

Once an individual has started along a truly spiritual path (as distinct from a religious one, or an occult one, or one involving some sort of spiritualism), his or her dreams will change their nature and leave the everyday, material dreams behind. Purifying dreams are likely to be experienced quite frequently: possibly the dream *Police* will appear more often; dreams of *Dirt*, or *Excrement*, or of the *Toilet*, or of walking or driving through *Mud*, will give some idea of the weight or extent of unwanted material that has become lodged in the *Personal unconscious mind*. Dreams of this nature may seem thoroughly unpleasant, but they are being realistic in their symbolism. If instead of following a spiritual path you practice serious *Meditation* or become deeply involved in religious fervour, your dreams may seem pleasant because they will have become *Wish-fulfilment dreams*, closing off the dark contents of the unconscious mind. Purification will not then be able to take place and the healthy *Cycle of the dreaming self* will cease.

Puzzlement *(A theme mood)*

There are so many of life's situations which are puzzling – any unsolved problem, in fact. But very often the mood of puzzlement can change during the course of a dream as a solution to whatever it is that is worrying you emerges. If you can recall the moment when this occurs, you will have a possible solution to the problem.

Q

QUARREL

Usually in a quarrel, both sides believe they are in the right and the other person is in the wrong. But it may be that neither side is in the right; or it may be that both sides are right, and simply using different sets of words and ideas to express the same truth: they will probably be using different *symbols* with a common interpretation. Dreaming about a real situation involving a quarrel usually means that the dreamer has made a misjudgement of some kind; to dream of a symbolic or allegorical quarrel in which you are taking part usually means that you, the dreamer, have been misled by your own pride. The *Inner feelings* see things as they are, without pride, and may be advising you to make amends if you have wronged somebody unintentionally.

See also: ABUSE; ACCUSATIONS; ANGER

QUEEN

If you are the queen in your dream

The regal figure you seem to have become in your dream may be representing yourself as you would like others to see you, and how you like to think of yourself. It could be a portrayal of your own *Persona*, your social mask which is becoming a little too powerful, a little too convincing for your own good.

If the dream queen is a person known to you

Plainly this person has made a very strong impression on your waking mind. Do you want her to behave like a queen? And what is your attitude towards her: admiration, worship, or servitude? The meaning of a dream such as this should be obvious to the dreamer. If it is not, it may be that the person who has become a queen in your dream, has something of real value to offer you, and you should not turn it down.

THE KEY TO DREAM ANALYSIS

If the dream queen is quite unknown to you

This dream figure could be one of the *Archetypes of the unconscious mind*. If you are a woman, she will have some very valuable advice to offer, and you need to study the dream carefully in order to discover exactly what it is. It will be related to your own recent waking experiences. If you are a man, this enigmatic dream figure could be the *anima*, the intuitive part of your own psyche that can help you to understand the female mind and your relationships with the opposite sex in particular. Again, your own recent experiences will help you interpret the dream.

See also: GODDESS; WISE PERSON

Questionnaire

When you are sharing your dreams with others who are helping with their interpretation, a dream questionnaire can be a great help. On your own too, you need to be objective about the different shades of meaning, and an impersonal questionnaire may help you in this respect. On your own you may well ignore seemingly trivial components of the dream, but they may hold significance which a questionnaire will bring out if answered thoroughly. Questions will raise issues such as: what does this thing in your dream mean to you personally? Have you ever owned one? Who or what does it remind you of? What colour was it? How was this dream person dressed? Did they wear a hat? What colour were their clothes? What do you remember about their features? What were they saying or doing? What were you doing at the time? Were you just watching or actually taking part? Where were you going in the dream? Where had you been? What were your surroundings like? What was the surface of the ground like? What buildings were to be seen?... and so on.

R

RAIL JOURNEY

If you normally commute by train

This will probably equate to your normal journey through life in the same way as *Driving*, the *Road*, or a *Path* usually does. It will probably be an everyday dream recalling or foretelling of encounters with friends, foes or colleagues.

If you very rarely travel by train

Where driving a car nowadays usually represents a mere extension of the legs, expressing your normal day-to-day journey through life, a rail journey is likely to signify a major transition. It implies being separated by a long distance, and travelling abroad or returning to your own country is often symbolised in dreams by a rail trip. Similarly it can symbolise a change of lifestyle rather than mere location. The imminent appearance in your life of someone from long ago or far away, or an associate with an unfamiliar approach to life, is often heralded by dreaming of their arrival by train. You may be meeting them at the station.

See also: JOURNEY

RAINBOW

This most beautiful of natural phenomena associated with the weather tends to appear against dark clouds when rainstorms are abating, and so inevitably it symbolises the end of a difficult period and the beginning of better times. It can also have a different meaning: As rainbow colours are the separate components of pure white light, they can represent divided parts of any whole. The human race with all its diverse people and cultures can be depicted in dreams in this way. It can symbolise people in general, different types represented by different colours. Someone in a dream who is shown as frightened of the rainbow is being portrayed as one who shuns society, or who is over-selective in his or her choice of associates.

See also: CLOUDS

Rapid eye movement

Also known as REM, it has often been said that dreams only occur during these periods of comparatively light sleep when the eyes beneath the eyelids are moving around. But this is a misconception: the deepest dreams seem to occur during the periods of deepest sleep. The most likely explanation is that these episodes of REM concern the 'lightest' dreams in the psychological and the spiritual sense. The most significant dreams, it will be discovered, are those which occur during the periods of deep sleep. It is during the REM state that outside influences can readily intrude on the dream. Memory even of REM dreams may not be perfect, of course, but *Dawn dreams* are recalled most vividly because the deep sleep cycle tends to precede waking. Such dreams usually bear no relationship to everyday concerns.

See also: Children's dreams

RATS

A few people like rats and keep them as pets, but the great majority see them as pests, suspect them of carrying diseases, and find them disgusting. The truth is, they are just animals trying to live their lives in peace, but their way of life inevitably brings them into close contact with humans. If a rat could speak, it would probably say that it would prefer to be domesticated, like a dog. As a dream symbol, the rat normally arouses strong feelings, as it does in real life. In fact a dream rat symbolises these feelings. Whatever the dreamer normally feels about rats, any real-life incident that invokes similar feelings may be expressed in a dream as an invasion of rats. The dream rat can become a symbol of your own behaviour if you have acted in what you yourself might consider to be a rat-like manner.

See also: ANIMALS

THE KEY TO DREAM ANALYSIS

Recording dreams

If you are to take your dream life seriously and venture a first step on the dream stairway, you will need to record your dreams. Don't rely on your memory: you may need to write down the details as soon as you wake, so a suitable notebook and pen or pencil should be within reach by the bed. A small notebook of the type that stays open where you want it to, and a ballpoint ready to write, these are important, as you may need to scrawl something down in the dark. Do not ignore seemingly trivial dreams, or anything that seems ridiculous or too cryptic – they may contain truths you need to know! Later, when you try to decipher what you have written, you can use the techniques of *Dream diagrams* or *Questionnaires*, or *Association of ideas* or *Free association*, When you have assembled enough dreams and their interpretations in sequence, you may wish to write them up neatly, not ignoring any details. The result will read like an autobiography of your inner life, progressing in tandem with the *World dream*.

Recurrent dreams

The same, or a very similar dream recurring again and again, like an old-fashioned gramophone with the needle stuck in one track: do you really need telling over and over? This type of dream is referring to something akin to a psychological block that is keeping you off balance and preventing progress. One note of warning: you may *dream* that a dream is recurrent when in fact it is not. Some people *say* that a dream is recurring when it is not, because they feel that recurrence adds weight or importance to it. *Warning dreams* of outside events are unlikely to recur: they are once for all events. A recurrent dream stems from within your own mind, and they are usually fairly uncomplicated. If you can interpret it, take it to heart, because it is a 'warning dream' of an *inside* event, needing urgent attention.

Re-entering a dream

This is a term used in group dream-therapy. When you feel that a dream has been cut short for some reason; if you feel that an important answer was about to emerge when you woke up; if you want to know *what happened next*, you might try dream re-entry. The technique is to relax and make yourself comfortable, with eyes closed, and feel as though you are drifting off to sleep while still remaining awake. The original dream will still be on your mind, and you visualize it, relive it, let it run its course in your mind, and when it reaches the 'end' allow it to continue as long as it will. The idea is not to make your dream lucid in the sense of manipulating it, but to quieten your own thoughts and feelings and allow it to run its full course without interference. Some dream workers like to prompt the dreamer to keep the dream on track, gently asking questions such as: 'what is happening now?' There is no reason why a person should not try this method on their own, but bear in mind that it is no use trying to control the dream yourself, or any conclusion will have arisen from your own desires. The technique is sometimes effective following a frightening dream, or recurrent dreams during which an unknown frightener seems about to appear. Re-entering such a dream may serve to identify the person or thing causing the disturbance, and may well bring to the surface the repressed memory of an alarming childhood experience.

Regression

A hypnotic procedure aimed at persuading a subject to 'regress' back to childhood and the point of birth and beyond, or before birth, in the hope of uncovering evidence of reincarnation (*see below*).

Reincarnation dreams

These are dreams in which the dreamer experiences an incident or series of incidents in the life (and often the death) of some real but usually completely unknown person who lived at some time in the past. Such dreams are normally very vivid and there is little doubt that they do feature real incidents in the lives of real people. Quite often they cross racial boundaries and involve matters about which the dreamer was previously ignorant. In this sense they are *Veridical dreams*. Some people go to great lengths to establish that the characters and the incidents are or were genuine, and take this as proof of reincarnation. But we might recall several equally vivid and completely true or veridical *Intuitive dreams* about usually traumatic incidents in the lives of real people – who are still alive and known to the dreamer. We might also be aware that on the level of the *Inner feelings* which are responsible for choosing our dream images, all people are linked: thoughts and feelings can be shared between people whose inner feelings have (to some extent) come to awareness. These dreams of others are also 'shared' in this sense, and they always seem to involve unpleasant emotions and traumatic incidents, often involving the death of the subject or others closely associated with them. To be on the receiving end of such dreams calls for sympathy, empathy, or compassion. Hypnotic regression (*see above*) is sometimes practiced in an attempt to strengthen or recapture such dreams, and there is always the risk of invoking *Wish-fulfilment dreams* if the mind or ego plays a part in this.

Relationship dreams

These are dreams centred around the dreamer's relationships with others, family, friends, colleagues or enemies. A general term, but if you use the *World dream* as your criterion you may conclude that relationship dreams cover the 'material' sector of everyday occurrences, the 'plant' sector of striving for an advantage, the 'animal' sector of morality and expanding influence, and scarcely reflecting the 'human' sector which is concerned more with personal development than with relationships. As one's dream-life develops, relationship dreams will become fewer.

Repression dreams

As a result of the *Cycle of the dreaming self*, matters which have long been buried in the *Personal unconscious mind* are sometimes pushed into awareness by way of dreams. When the cyclic process is well under way, such matters may come to awareness without the help of dreams. A repression dream brings to awareness a long-forgotten incident usually from childhood, a traumatic incident perhaps which was not accepted at the time by the conscious mind, and pushed or repressed into the 'subconscious'. It may well have formed part of the *Shadow* if it had remained repressed, only to emerge in the form of nameless fears or nightmares, perhaps as a demon or a monster.

RIVER   *Running water*

The flow of emotions, or of sexual desires, or even of life itself. In the religious sense it can represent the Holy Spirit, and several real-life rivers in the world have religious significance to many people. In their dreams the river will represent their own fulfilment or hopes for the future. To Christians, the Jordan River for centuries has represented the barrier between life and death. The image of living on the banks of a river may represent someone who is suppressing his or her sexual desires. To someone on the path of spiritual purification, or of psychic completion, the dream symbol of a river may be seen as something to be crossed, sooner or later. On a more mundane level, a dream river that is in flood symbolises turbulent sexual feelings of which the dreamer is rather afraid. A gentle flow of clear water implies that one's conscience is clear.

See also: FORD; BRIDGE; WATER

ROAD   *The way along which you and others travel*

The course of your life is often depicted in dreams as a road along which you travel. The surface of the road may be smooth, or pot-holed, or muddy, or rock-strewn, symbolising the obstacles you meet from day to day. The dream road may be narrow or broad, straight or winding. Everything and everyone you encounter on your dream journey reflects the incidents that happen to you in real life, and need to be interpreted accordingly.

See also: DRIVING; JOURNEY; PATH; RAIL JOURNEY

ROCKS *or stones*

A rocky, stony place that you have to travel through usually represents temporary hardships in real life that you have to endure. Rocks are always a symbol of solid materiality, lacking in spiritual content, and this can be taken in numerous ways. The symbol can refer to other uncaring people who are making life difficult, or to matters of health that cause you problems. It can imply that you are lacking in or would benefit from greater spiritual motivation and need to look beyond mere material or financial profit and loss. Something similar is implied by a solitary towering rock in your dream: it is a symbol of the *Self* – your own psychic centre, which has become rock-bound and inflexible through excessive materiality. The dream might be advising you to be less hard and unyielding in your outlook.

See also: *Cycle of creation in dreams;* MOUNTAIN; ROAD; STONE CIRCLE

RUINS   *A building no longer in use*

Rather a poignant symbol, reflecting past glories and certainties long gone. But a building can also symbolise oneself, or some other person, and a ruined building can represent someone on whom you used to rely, but is no longer available: a parent, perhaps. It can also represent an organization of some kind, which is no longer to be depended upon, or attitudes which belong to the past and cannot be recaptured.

See also: ABBEY; *Self*

S

Sadness   (A theme mood)

The feeling of sadness remembered, or experienced after you wake from a dream is often associated with *Intuitive dreams* or so-called *Reincarnation dreams*, in either of which you will have experienced at first hand the genuine feelings of another person during the traumatic incident which transferred itself to your own dreaming awareness. In any other type of dream sadness may be associated with feelings of guilt, or perhaps genuine grief at something you have experienced, some *Trigger event*. If sadness is being 'cleared out' of your *Personal unconscious mind* it may be related to some long past event when you were unable to express grief at the time, and need to clear it out of your system.

SAND

The earth, the soil, represents the material background to our lives, and sand is totally barren. When life-giving water falls on sand usually it either drains away very quickly or forms a quagmire, and any life form will find it very difficult to survive there. To dream you are struggling through sandy desert implies a complete lack of power, or any sense of power. When you consider the *World dream* and refer also to *Adlerian dreams* you will see that plants struggling to take roothold in the desert are like humans striving after a modicum of power for themselves – people who are feeling helpless in the face of overwhelming odds. Nobody likes a pushy person, but perhaps the dream symbol is telling you to be more assertive in your dealings with others; it is no use depending on their goodwill.

See also: DESERT; SWAMP

SCRAPHEAP

A collection of junk and old items that people no longer have use for. They may perhaps be recyclable and turned into something useful, but they are not items you want cluttering up your house. The _Self_ is sometimes symbolised in dreams as a house, and it may be that this junk consists of old ideas, bad habits, past values, worn-out relationships that are no longer relevant to your life. It is time they were cleared out, and your lifestyle given an airing.

See also: LUGGAGE; OBSTACLES; PIT

SEA

If you are connected with the sea in your everyday life, to dream of the sea may be simply placing the dream on an everyday basis. But if there is no obvious connection, remember that water symbolises human emotions, including the sexual urges. The other features and people in the dream should give you the clue. You may be swimming or merely paddling in these powerful feelings. You may be out of your depth and drowning in them. You may be able to float over them with impunity; you may even be able to swallow the whole sea, to imply that you have risen above and can well cope with all these emotional passions. The sea can also symbolise the unfathomable *Collective unconscious mind*, and if your dream is a *Dawn dream*, a *Great dream* perhaps, this may be the significance of it. Swim in this sea with caution: remember that everything it contains are collective phenomena and not your own personal contents. To believe otherwise is to court psychological inflation and long-term disillusionment.

See also: DROWNING; WATER

Selection of images

If you think of yourself as being made up of various constituents: your outer personality: the ego or personal driving force; the brain with its thoughts; the 'heart' with its emotions; and your inner or hidden personality which makes up the unconscious mind: the *Inner feelings*; the *Persona*; the *Shadow*; you will see that all these factors are taken into consideration when your dream images are being selected. The part which has the final say in this selection process is that which we call the inner feelings, because it has access not only to your own past experiences, your thoughts and feelings and problems, but also to the *Collective unconscious* – the great sea of past experiences and subtle solutions to mysteries common to the whole of mankind. Everything that your conscious mind has pondered over, or perhaps rejected or backed away from, is compared, matched, blended into a recognisable form, and re-presented by the inner feelings in the form of dreams, often with a psychological or purely practical solution to whatever has been troubling you.

See also: *Mandala diagrams*

Self

In dreams it is possible to stand back and observe yourself. It may be you with your normal appearance, possibly in the past or in the future. It may be you flying, or floundering. This gives you a chance to see yourself and your actions objectively. It may be your innocent self without the trappings of personality and acquired characteristics – a baby or young child emerged from the *Collective unconscious*, looking at what goes on in the world. Or it may be yourself in the guise of a house, sometimes a great mansion, with numerous servants who may well be portrayed as undisciplined and neglectful: your base passions and desires. Downstairs in the basement a *Demon* may lurk, and the master of the house may be somewhere upstairs in his study, unaware of the chaos that reigns in his house. Or the self may be seen as a farm where all sorts of possibilities are nurtured. Or again the self may be seen as a *Mandala* design formed in any number of ways: you may be a flower, or perhaps a water lily floating on a pond. All this is a reminder that when you begin to record and understand your dreams, they will almost all be centred around you, and your own unconscious contents. This may seem selfish or self-centred, but it has been said that you cannot begin to change the world until you have first changed yourself, and that change has to come from within.

See also: *Mandala diagrams; Spherical symbols of the self*

Sexual dreams

You do not normally dream of your own sex life or your attitude towards sex, unless there is some kind of sexual imbalance or dissatisfaction within yourself. If you are quite happy in all respects with your sexual contents and the way in which you cope with your own sexual instincts, you ought not to be dreaming about them. Sexual dreams, then, tend to point to some need for a change of habits, possibly a more open outlook as regards *Morality*. Beware of hurting people's feelings by criticising their sexual habits: by upsetting them you may be upsetting your own psychic balance.

Shadow

If we study the *Cycle of the dreaming self* and the *Spherical symbols of self* we will gain some idea of the unconscious processes within our own mind. Anything that we have found too unpleasant for whatever reason to accept, thoughts, feelings, ideas, observations, experiences, we tend to push them away into the *Pit*, into the *Personal unconscious mind*, and if they are too horrendous for the *Inner feelings* to process and re-present in a more acceptable form, they remain there, sinking as though by the force of gravity into the lowest and darkest part of the unconscious mind. This is the source of what are usually called *Nightmares*, for sooner or later these unpleasant contents are liable to force their attention on the conscious mind in symbolic form – as monsters, demons, witches, the devil, the personification of everything the dreamer detests. When the shadow emerges in dream, the dreamer on waking will probably fail to recognise this dreadful apparition as his or her own, and it can indeed be very frightening indeed. But it is one of those things about which we say: 'better out than in!' When we pay attention to our dreams and accept the bad as well as the good as our own and part of ourselves, these dark contents can be evicted, bit by bit, never to return.

Sharing of dreams

Of course dreams can be shared in the sense of telling others about them and asking their opinions, and this is covered in the sections on

Group dream therapy, *Acting out the dream*, and *Enacting dreams in company*. But dreams can also be shared on an intuitive level, in several different ways. Two people who are emotionally close to one another may experience the same dream; the *Collective intelligence* can insure that one person is forewarned and forearmed ready to interpret a friend's dream; you may experience traumatic incidents in another's life by way of a dream, and they may do the same with regards to you, as in *Inter-reactive dreams*. Within families dreams are shared probably far more often than most of us realise.

SKELETON

This framework of bones is a term used to mean the basic material framework of almost anything, not merely the remains of a human being, but the basic layout of any scheme, material or abstract, before the details have been added. So in a non-human or non-animal context, it symbolises the raw beginnings of some project that may be developed into something substantial. In the human and animal sense, however, it symbolises the last remaining traces of what was once a living, functioning being. Usually, as a dream symbol, it refers to the latter: the mortal remains of what was once a living, breathing, possibly spiritual person. A *memento mori*, if you find a skeleton in your dream it probably refers to human relationships and influence now long gone.

See also: ARCHAEOLOGY; BONES; CORPSE

SNAKE

An ancient symbol in many cultures, and with several different meanings. In the biblical Book of Genesis the snake is the first tempter of mankind, offering judgment and intelligence instead of a purely instinctive way of life. A snake might symbolise eternal youth, or even eternal life, as indicated by the sloughing of its skin. It is a symbol of untrustworthiness because of the way in which it may slither unseen through the grass, a hidden danger. It can symbolise lust, through its sinuous, phallic shape. A dream snake seems to be offering a warning not to trust somebody or something – or could it be you, the dreamer, who is acting in this way?

See also: ANIMALS

SNOW AND ICE

Fortunately, snow and ice melt after a while when warmer weather arrives. As a dream symbol the implication is that the emotional atmosphere surrounding the dreamer is cold and frosty. Walking through cold, snowy conditions implies that the dreamer can expect times to be difficult and somewhat uncomfortable for a while, though an improvement will take place before long. A dream with snow seems to be advising the dreamer to be patient. A child's dream of snow, on the other hand, may speak only of pleasure and not hardship.

See also: FROST; GLACIER

Spherical symbols of the self

The *Self* can be symbolised by a *Mandala*, which is frequently round, often square, sometimes a combination of both. When considering the self in relation to dreams, and the constantly recurrent *Cycle of the dreaming self* it is useful to think in terms of a circle, or more correctly a globe, an orb like the earth itself. The upper half is bathed in sunshine, and below the 'equator' or horizon, all is in darkness. This represents the conscious and the unconscious mind respectively. The Chinese symbol of *Yin and yang* expresses the same principle. The *Mandala diagrams* of the dreaming process are spherical symbols of the self. They could be superimposed on a larger circle representing the collective sphere with which the *Inner feelings* is able to have contact, as a circle within a circle, or a wheel within a wheel. The upper half of this surrounding circle will represent the spiritual dimension as it applies to humans; the lower half will represent the *Collective unconscious*, from which *Archetypes* of the unconscious mind may emerge and feature in our more significant, *Great dreams*. This greater sphere, though impersonal and unapproachable by the personality, can still be considered as part of the self.

STATUE

The likeness of a person carved in stone or some other material – this could be a representation of the *Self*, or of some aspect of the self that has become petrified and frozen with disuse, possibly one of the *Archetypes of the unconscious mind*. Someone who has been behaving in what the rest of the world perceives as an outrageous manner will seem to be out of touch with the sensitivities of others: perhaps his or her *Persona* has taken on this symbolically uncaring or uncooperative form. A solitary standing stone may carry much the same significance. Whether the dream symbol refers to the dreamer personally or to some other figure, the person concerned seems to be lacking in emotional rapport. When the dream statue is of some famous figure from the past, it could be that the dreamer has been taking an interest in or attaching undue importance to matters which are no longer valid. There could be a phallic significance, particularly when the statue becomes small enough to be held in the hand.

See also: CARVINGS; IDOL

STEPPING STONES *A way to cross water dry-footed*

In dreams a stream to be crossed usually represents the flow of emotions and sexual attraction, which in this case the dreamer feels needs to be resisted. Wading or swimming across means that the dreamer is sampling these powerful feelings without becoming too greatly influenced by them. Crossing by means of a *Bridge* implies that he or she wishes to avoid contact with these emotions altogether. Stepping stones represent a convenient middle way: one is close enough to the water to study it carefully and take an interest in it, yet still remain, or hope to remain, unaffected by the flow of feelings which it symbolises.

See also: FORD; RIVER; WATER

THE KEY TO DREAM ANALYSIS

STONE CIRCLE   *A circular ancient monument*

Prehistoric stone monuments are widespread in parts of Europe and particularly perhaps in the British Isles. It is in Ireland, Wales, England and Scotland that the dream symbol of the stone circle is sometimes experienced. Stonehenge is a famous but not at all typical example: most of them are simply rough circles of rocks to be found in hilly country and wild areas. Whatever the motives of the people who constructed them, in dreams they can be seen as a *Mandala* of the *Self*, particularly in its relation to the world and the solar system. It can also signify the family circle, especially when this tends to be hidebound and unyielding. People who have been seeking a spiritual 'way' may dream of having to pass through the circle in some way, arriving at a new level of understanding.

See also: ARCHAEOLOGY; DOOR; ROCKS

STORE

A building or container filled with all sorts of goods may represent the *Personal unconscious mind*, the place normally hidden and closed where all your experiences and impressions are stored. To visit and rummage through this store in your dream is good: it implies that the *Cycle of the dreaming self* is working well. But a store or shop may also symbolise materiality – the 'lowest' end of the spiritual hierarchy, but the place where all sorts of good things are available. If you are on the way 'down' you may arrive at this store with a feeling of expectation. If you are on the way 'up' and following a spiritual path, you will be leaving this store behind.

See also: BARN

Submission of will

Dreams are produced by the *Inner feelings*, which are part of the *Personal unconscious mind*. In dreams they deal with all the matters which have not been finalized by the conscious mind, reassemble them and re-present them in the form of dreams acceptable to your waking mind. The process cannot really be made conscious, and if the will or the ego intrudes into a dream, as happens sometimes during a *Lucid dream* or in a *Wish-fulfilment dream*, the cycling or clearing-out process will stop. The will is an indispensable tool of the whole person, but it cannot deal with matters which arrive from a spiritual source, that is, from *above* the limits of the human capacity. This also applies to what we might call the highest part of our own *Self*: Deep insights such as this can only be received when the will, or conscious intent, is in a state of submission and ceases to function – if only temporarily. This is what should happen during sleep. From time to time It has been recommended to apply the will before sleeping, in an effort to induce some special sort of dream, as in *Incubating dreams* or *Encouraging dreams*, and of course it is for the individual to decide: but because I believe that dreams are meant to teach us something, and not the other way round, this book advises against the practice.

See also: Ego overruled in a dream

SUN

As the prime giver of life to the earth, the sun must be one of the most ancient of dream symbols. The rising sun equates to a new dawn, new hopes, new possibilities, the rebirth of the psyche to a new understanding, a new level of being. Dark deeds are uncovered by the sun, so it is a symbol of openness and honesty. Wealth and material success are symbolised by sunshine. Darkness speaks of death and disaster, loss of health and wealth. But a setting sun rarely predicts disaster: it marks the passing of the established order and promises peace and respite. Where danger lurks the arrival of darkness can also symbolise safety. It is so very basic a symbol that when it features in a dream it is probably merely highlighting whatever the dream itself portrays.

See also: ECLIPSE

THE KEY TO DREAM ANALYSIS

SUNDIAL

The dial itself is a *Mandala* symbol, probably representing the *Self* under the influence of time: the march of progress and the inevitability of fate. The upright pedestal is an ancient phallic symbol, probably less in evidence nowadays than when people were less open about their sexual desires, but still a potent symbol of regeneration and the continuity of life. The sundial suggests a certain closeness to nature and a clinging to old ways. The time it shows is the only true time known to nature, the time based on the movements of our planet in relation to the sun, rather than the sophisticated averaged-out time of modern civilization. As a dream symbol, like a clock, the sundial can express urgency and the transitory nature of life. It can represent a kind of memorial to past times and people who are no longer alive. It can suggest the necessity for peace and tranquillity, and above all it can represent an ancient set of values that is still valid, and which would be of great benefit to the dreamer.

See also: CALENDAR; CLOCK

Symbolic nature of dreams

Purely material dreams of an everyday nature, referring to relationships and recent events, may appear almost completely devoid of what we have come to think of as dream symbols, but they invariably show a new aspect or a different take on events which makes them symbolic rather than realistic. Once the *Development of dreams* begins – which it will when you start recording and paying attention to them, dreams may seem to have become wholly symbolic because they no longer refer to everyday events. The *Cycle of the dreaming self* will have begun in earnest and the unwanted contents of the *Personal unconscious mind* will be moulded into recognisable forms by the *Inner feelings*. These contents when they sink into the unconscious mind are fragmentary, jumbled and confused, and to re-present them in a way acceptable to the conscious mind entails the use of symbols. A dream story is an allegory, comparable perhaps to the parables told by Jesus. They paint a picture on one scale, of events and consequences relating to a different scale; as is the nature of symbols, they present abstract matters in material terms.

Symbols and their origin

Take any material object: what does it mean to you in the abstract? And what are all the incidents you can remember from the past, relating to that object? That material object is a symbol for you of all the answers you have come up with. A symbol may have any number of meanings. When we try to understand the *Inner feelings* which belong to the personal unconscious mind, we may realise that this 'higher emotional centre' is able to communicate with others on the same deep level, the level beneath our normal awareness. These inner feelings, being non-material, 'think' in the abstract, and they have access not only to the contents of your own *Personal unconscious mind* with an overview of your whole life, but also to the *Collective unconscious* and the symbols that apply to the whole human race. Shared symbols that come to our own awareness include the *Archetypes of the unconscious mind*, which are able to take on a form and appearance that will be understood by you personally.

See also: Spherical symbols of the self

T

Tearfulness   *(A theme mood)*

Sorrow as the background to a dream is usually referring a psychological block - a refusal on the dreamer's part to accept his or her own contents. We each have our own nature, our own unique inheritance giving us a basic character over which we have no control. When we feel that our 'true nature' is less than acceptable we may try to hide it. We may unconsciously strengthen our *Persona* at the expense of truth, forever putting on a false front in case others think badly of us. There is an ancient saying: *In vino veritas*, which implies that when we drop our guard or lose our inhibitions we may be seen without disguise. The *inner feelings* have no inhibitions, and see things as they really are; in sleep we drop our guard. The dream may be telling us to be more open and accept our own true nature.

TEETH

When you have toothache you might dream of something unpleasant happening to your teeth – a quite understandable reaction when pain is nagging at your conscious awareness, even in your sleep. But many people dream that their teeth are broken or missing when they are perfectly sound. A person who is said to be 'toothless' is unable to react as he or she would like, and this is the probable implication of toothlessness as a dream symbol. Perhaps somebody has been provoking the dreamer in real life, taking advantage of the apparent lack of retaliation.

See also: BULLY

Terror   *(A theme mood)*

Your dream may not seem to be about frightening things; it may be an apparently ordinary *Relationship dream*, but you wake in a cold sweat. Terror may of course feature in a real *Nightmare*, but if there is no obvious source of fear the dream details should give you the clue. You may be alarmed at the seemingly unprovoked aggression displayed by known or unknown characters featuring in your dream. Only you, the dreamer, know all the facts leading up to the dream, and the *Trigger events* that prompted it. There may be a very good reason why you want to keep something private – but it certainly seems that there is something you don't want the other characters in your dream to find out about.

THEATRE

A theatrical performance is not the place to look for sincerity, and the point about actors is that while going about their daily occupation they are pretending to be something or somebody which they are not. It is also a place of entertainment, however, so theatrical deception is unlikely to be malicious. A dream theatre is not representing truth, and though the characters in it are not to be taken at their face value, they may be offering a new perspective on an old problem, suggesting a light-hearted attitude towards the possibility of tolerating problematic circumstances which cannot be dealt with in any other way.

See also: ACTING

THORNS

Prickly bushes and the like represent a hostile environment, full of difficulties or minor dangers. They can symbolise persecution and unfair discrimination when this is being experienced. A beautiful rose bush also bears thorns, and in this and other similar cases the thorns will represent the inconveniences and snags or annoyances which may beset you before you can attain whatever it is that you desire.

See also: CACTUS; OBSTACLES

THE KEY TO DREAM ANALYSIS

THRONE   *The seat of majesty*

If you are seated on the throne

There seems to be something not quite right about the idea of seeing yourself enthroned in splendour. You are plainly being symbolised as superior over others, but in what way? Search the dream very carefully for clues, because clearly you cannot sit on the throne with sincerity.

If someone you know is seated on the throne

This person may genuinely have something of great value to offer if you are prepared to accept their superiority in some regard. On the other hand, this may simply be *your* opinion of what you suppose *their* opinion of themselves to be.

If a stranger is sitting on the throne

The dream needs exploring carefully for further clues. It may be that the person sitting on the throne is one of the *Archetypes of the unconscious mind*, in which case the message they convey may be of the greatest value to your waking mind.

See also: KING; QUEEN

TIDAL WAVE   *A wall of water or a tsunami*

A great wave of emotion, and more particularly an immense surge of sexual desires, these are things over which we have little control, and if they are worrying us we are liable to dream of them in this way. If you are confronted with a great wall of water about to engulf you in a dream, note particularly what effect it had, not only on you but on any other people and objects round about. If you are swept away and find yourself in difficulties, it seems that an urgent reappraisal of your lifestyle is overdue. If however it leaves you unaffected and dry, though other characters nearby may be swept away, the dream message is that although the way ahead may prove daunting and difficult at times, you will eventually overcome your problems.

See also: DROWNING; WATER

TOILET

It is quite a common dream experience: you need to go to the toilet fairly urgently, but cannot find one that is usable: it doesn't work, it's not properly plumbed in, it's too dirty, or too much in the public gaze. In other words, your body wants to get rid of your waste material, but can't. There may be a very simple and practical explanation: you want to go without bothering to wake up, and your *Inner feelings* are pointing out that you can't do that. But if you don't really need to go that badly, there may be quite another reason for the dream: the waste matter you need to get rid of may be psychological clutter, or perhaps bad habits and faults which are holding you back and blocking the free *Cycle of the dreaming self*. You know you ought to get rid of them, but it is far easier to find excuses for hanging on. There are no moral implications in this; the dream is simply drawing your attention to the state of affairs existing within your own psyche.

See also: EXCREMENT

TOWER   *A tall strong building*

There are several types of tower of course. There is the tower block of flats which can merely set the scene for an everyday *Relationship dream*. Or when someone is setting out in business and is somewhat nervous of the potential competition, he or she may dream of towering office blocks and industrial buildings which make the dreamer feel small. Commonly, however, a stout tower represents the family, or marriage. A 'tower of strength' on which we ought to be able to rely, and inside which we can hide if needs be. You may dream you are outside such a building and wandering how you can get in, because you have been searching for security in real life. Inside the tower, you may still be exploring, perhaps dreading what is in the cellar or the dungeons below ground, and wishing perhaps that you could gain access to the uppermost rooms. This is because most people live in one dimension, above their own *Personal unconscious mind* and below their own higher psychological and spiritual possibilities.

See also: Self

TREASURE

If you have actually found treasure in your dream

If you have not recently had a stroke of good fortune and thus know what the symbol means, you need to think through the dream details carefully to find out its true nature.

If you are searching for the treasure which you know to be near

The dream is probably referring to a spiritual or psychological treasure which is already present within your own psyche. If another person known to you features in the dream, he or she will have been or is about to be instrumental in helping you find the treasure. When you start to record and pay attention to your dreams, you will know that a great treasure is the ultimate discovery: there can be few treasures on earth more important than the discovery of your own soul.

See also: DRAGON; GOLD; JEWELS; PEARL

Trigger events

Events in your life consist of all the experiences you meet with, things that happen, people you meet. Any of these may serve to trigger a dream because it is in some way acting as a catalyst within your own *Personal unconscious mind,* linking up and serving to bring together otherwise disjointed and disconnected memories, ideas, worries, hopes and fears, and making sense of them. *Repression dreams* may be triggered by some apparently chance encounter, bringing back matters which were long forgotten by your conscious mind, but which hold great psychological significance, traumatic incidents perhaps which happened during childhood, and which have been causing you problems ever since, beneath the threshold of awareness. *Waking inspirations* too may come to you as a result of trigger events, particularly when the *Cycle of the dreaming self* is clearing out some of the debris within our unconscious minds.

Trivial dreams

Some dreams when interpreted really do seem trivial, even when they are obviously not *Dozing dreams*, or *Evening dreams*, nor even *Relationship dreams* about matters which might be thought unimportant. But *Everyday dreams* are a reality, and one's mind cannot hope to understand all the processes that go in inside the *Personal unconscious mind*. It sometimes happens that you can find nothing of value to be learnt. Pride is a harmful emotion which can cloak the truth, and patience is indeed a virtue. Allow the *Inner feelings* to be the best judge of what should be known by way of dreams.

TUNNEL   *Travelling underground*

The road or path symbolises your own journey through life, and when this plunges below ground or runs through a patch of darkness, you have temporarily lost sight of your surroundings or the way ahead. If in your dream you were aware of a glimmer of light ahead, your position will soon be made plain and new understanding is sure to ensue. If not, and when all analysis yields no further clues, patience and a sense of submission is called for. It may be portraying a real situation at work or in society where you are running through a difficult patch. Or it may represent your own *Personal unconscious mind* where your normal thought processes can see nothing. If this dream is persistent and worrying, it may be pointing ahead to a temporary loss of full normal consciousness. Tunnels don't go on forever, and any trauma of this nature will probably prove to be a temporary glitch.

See also: ABYSS; DARKNESS

U

UNEMPLOYMENT

Real unemployment, or a feeling of having nothing useful to do, no useful function to perform, can have a depressing effect. An economic depression in the country can result in a rise in clinical depression among the people, and a play on words like this is frequently to be found in dreams. When somebody is feeling depressed, they may well dream of unemployment, though they have no shortage of work in fact. A major cause of depression is an awareness of one's inability to follow the inner self: one's true nature may not fit in with the lifestyle one is obliged to lead, for whatever reason. Everyone is unique, and the only way by which one can reach higher awareness – especially spiritual attainment – is being true to one's own self. To 'atone' means being 'at one' in every sense. A dream of unemployment may be telling you to be true or honest to your own inner character: 'Know then thyself!'

See also: LOST; *Self*

UNIFORM   *Conforming in dress*

Dressing uniformly is a token of involvement, or belonging to a certain class or group. Even a 'fashion uniform' means that you are associating yourself with others of a similar turn of mind. At school, in the services, and various types of employment, a uniform represents equality and conformity. If you wear a uniform in real life, this could be called your normal dress. But if you dream of wearing a uniform when this is not the case, it implies that you have been acting in the way that others expect you to act, or are being forced into the same fate as others. This is particularly significant if you consider yourself an individualist and like to be different. Perhaps your individuality is being compromised.

See also: CLOTHES

V

VALLEY

Solid earth represents materiality – the substance of the *World dream*, and to dream you are in a valley implies that you are penned in by a material situation. When the valley is shrouded in *Mist* or *Fog*, you will be unable to see your way clearly, either to go on or to go back. The dream symbol may be referring to a matter of physical health, when you are helpless to do anything about it; or it might refer to a dead-end situation at work, or confines of some kind from which there is no easy escape. If you cannot think of any parallel in real life, take it as a friendly warning: If you have had anything to do with the occult, or spiritualism, it would be better for you to turn your back on these things, and seek a more truly spiritual influence in your life.

See also: JOURNEY; ROAD; ROCKS

VASE *or similar ornamental container*

The concept of a personal vase which you would like people to admire, or in which you can place flowers to beautify your surroundings, is closely related to the concept of the *Persona*, which represents that part or aspect of yourself that you would like others to see; the way in which you would like them to think of you. But the vase is more personal and individual than that: it is only meant to be seen and admired by those close to you whom you particularly wish to impress. As a dream symbol it crops up chiefly in romantic situations.

See also: BARN; CUP; STORE

Veridical dreams

This is a term applied to dreams during which you dream of previously unknown facts, incidents, places and people, all of which later turn out to be completely true. The experience is closely allied to an *Intuitive dream*, or a dream in which the *Collective intelligence* is involved. Always of great interest, such dreams usually follow some traumatic incident involving not the dreamer but the subject of the dream, or a close emotional involvement between the subject and the dreamer. They are frequently *Dawn dreams*, and depend upon the principles of empathy, sympathy, and compassion on the part of the dreamer, which in their turn depend on a well-balanced psyche.

VOLCANO

The symbolic mountain that 'blows its top' describes a material and apparently peaceful situation that is liable to turn dangerous if taken too much for granted. It may feature within marriage, or at work, or any situation where other people's feelings and patience may be stretched to the limit.

See also: EARTHQUAKE

Volitional dreams

A dream involving the dreamers' own willpower, a deliberately induced dream intended to supply information – this represents a dream-trip to nowhere. The hidden *Inner feelings* select the images and symbols intended to make up your dreams, clearing out the clutter of rejected or worrying thoughts and impressions within your own *Personal unconscious mind*. The higher emotional centre known as the inner feelings cannot be coerced. If the mind or ego try to take part in the dreaming process, the *Cycle of the dreaming self* will simply cease to function, and the resultant dreams will probably be mere exercises in imagination, and of no psychological value.

Waking dreams

A situation in which real-life events fall into place in symbolic terms in order to portray some particular truth or exchange an important intuitional piece of information. Dreams are normally arranged and their symbols or images selected by the *Inner feelings* acting beneath the level of awareness. Waking dreams are real-life situations arranged by the inner feelings when this higher emotional centre is functioning within the level of awareness. They will usually involve what is popularly known as 'second sight'.

Waking inspirations

Dream solutions to some problem usually occur in the form of a *Dawn dream*. A waking inspiration stems from the same source involving the *Inner feelings*, but occurs when the subject is awake – usually during a quiet period when thoughts and emotions are temporarily in abeyance. The inspiration or sudden brainwave will have arisen unexpectedly and spontaneously from the 'subconscious', specifically from the *Personal unconscious mind.*.

WALL *A solid barrier*

A dream wall may be a barrier to your progress, but it may be simply a guide to steer you along the best path. There may be a way through or over the wall if you follow it. Your current course through life was quite probably in question, and a barrier may turn out to be either a hindrance or a help. Although it may refer to something in the nature of a psychological barrier impeding your forward progress, or a hindrance set up by uncooperative people in real life, a wall can be a safety measure too, blocking off a dangerous path.

See also: HEDGE; FENCE; GATEWAY; LABYRINTH

Warning dreams

There seems to be something desirable about dreams that deliver a timely warning, and many people long to experience them, even trying to induce them (see *Volitional dreams*), or make themselves believe that their *Everyday dreams* are warning them about future events. But true warning dreams are usually very private and personal, involving family and friends, and relating to matters of personal concern. The *Inner feelings* are not normally concerned with general events, however important they may seem: these inner feelings within the *Personal unconscious mind* are concerned with personal psychic growth, and are not interested in 'proving themselves' by producing amazing results or forecasting events of international significance.

WATER

The flow of emotions

There are many forms that the water symbol can take – the sea, waves, rivers, streams, lakes, ponds, or wells, or drinking water in a cup or the hollow of the hand, or even the mere sound of water trickling. Personal interpretation of the whole dream should never be neglected, even if the meaning of the symbol itself seems obvious. The feelings or the emotions are symbolised in dreams by water, and it follows that the clarity or murkiness of the dream water is significant. Psychological clutter that has not yet been dealt with in the *Personal unconscious mind* and feelings of guilt that have not been in some way atoned will darken and discolour the water with mud. Clear water, perhaps with coral, shells and clean pebbles signifies crystal-clear emotions, a clear conscience, with not too many psychological blocks. Murky water featuring in your dream-life suggests that you should begin to take your own inner condition seriously, beginning by recording and analysing your dreams assiduously. The first step towards solving a problem is acknowledging that a problem exists.

Sexual desire symbolised by water

In the traditional symbolism of the East a hermit living on the banks of a mighty river represents one who practices celibacy. The river represents his sexual desires, and he is able to watch it rolling past without wishing to plunge in. But when this determination arises from the will, it has been pointed out that when the will evaporates on death, the river will wash away the hermit's remains. In western symbolism a river can represent death, and finally crossing this river implies leaving behind one's life and all the desires associated with it: birth, sex, and death are all closely related in the world of symbolism, and of course they are closely related in the world of nature too. To dream of experiencing difficulties in crossing a river or stream, implies that you are reluctant to abandon emotional attachments, and in particular old sexual habits that you might be better off without. It can also mean that the dreamer is unwilling to face his or her own emotions when these seem too deep, and tends to switch off and become detached when emotional subjects are raised. Perhaps your dream is advising you to listen sympathetically to other people's emotional problems.

The lake of the inner self

A lake, a pond, any restricted area of water is likely to symbolise the inner self, or more specifically the unseen and unfathomable depths of the personal unconscious mind. A flower such as a water lily floating on the surface as a dream image could be pointing out that the dreamer has been placing too much reliance on his or her intellect; possibly by practising self control and following moral restrictions which might be better relaxed. No-one should neglect the deep water of the unconscious mind while seeing only the water lily of conscious awareness above. In the depth of this dream lake lurks the *Shadow*, gaining in strength and feeding on the detritus that floats to the bottom. The personal unconscious mind may also be symbolised by a well, which carries the idea of a store of wisdom waiting to be drawn from this well and drunk. To dream of drinking water implies that you are taking in whatever is being symbolised by the water – in this case, overcoming personal problems through the *Cycle of the dreaming self*.

THE KEY TO DREAM ANALYSIS

The collective unconscious symbolised by water

A vast ocean rather than a pond, this is a symbol of the *Collective unconscious* which, although available to the *Inner feelings* is shared equally by the whole of humankind. This is a sea of wisdom, and the source of the *Archetypes of the unconscious mind* which can impart the best advice, but although it is good to become familiar with its contents it can be dangerous to swim in this sea. People have become possessed, as it were, by images from the collective unconscious, falsely believing them to be personal attributes. A gentle sip of water from this great sea, on the other hand, is only ever beneficial: a taste of wisdom whilst appreciating good advice.

See also: BOAT; BRIDGE; DAM; FORD; LAKE; RIVER; STEPPING STONES; TIDAL WAVE

WEEDING

Particularly if you ever practice gardening in real life, you may recognise weeding as a dream image, possibly with no other symbols involved in the dream. When we become aware of the need to shed the various faults and weaknesses that have invaded the territory of the *Inner feelings*, and on discovering that it is impossible to do this using the mind and emotions in the usual way, we are liable to dream of weeding a flower bed. Invasive plants with long underground roots, weeds becoming matted inextricably in the roots of prize plants, weeds which sprawl over the top of other plants and smother them, these are succinct images. A great deal of tweaking and gentle separation of invasive roots is needed, and this is a symbol of the work done by the inner feelings during the purifying *Cycle of the dreaming self.*

See also: DIRT; EXCREMENT

White lie dreams

A dream which falls in this category is, in effect, a *Warning dream* of a personal nature that seems to bear all the hallmarks of a true warning dream: it may be advising the dreamer to take or avoid taking certain action and giving reasons that appear to be valid – e.g., avoid travelling to an appointment as planned because an accident was due to happen along the way. After the dreamer has followed this advice in good faith, it transpires that there was no accident situation, but another far more subtle reason why they should *not* attend that particular interview. This would be a 'white lie' – a deliberate untruth told with good intent, something that is quite acceptable to the *Inner feelings*, and indeed to the whole field of spirit. The mysterious *Collective intelligence* may well be involved in the formation of this type of dream.

WISE PERSON   *An unknown person who gives advice*

If a real person known to the dreamer gives them the benefit of his or her advice in a dream, the value of that advice is certainly in question. But the unknown wise person is likely to be one of the so-called *Archetypes of the unconscious mind*, representing the highest, intuitive part of the dreamer's own psyche. In this case the advice will be sound, though the dream will need careful interpretation according to the dreamer's own experiences and needs. This dream figure may appear as a well-dressed bystander of authority, a doctor, or a teacher, or possibly the dreamer's own father. The wise person is closely allied to the dream figures of the *King*, the *Queen*, and the *Hero*. There is an example of this in the section on *Dream diagrams*, in the example dream, when the dreamer's own 'wise person' travels with him in his car and gives him good advice when needed.

Wish fulfilment dreams

When somebody wishes fervently for some outcome, or has fears about their fate, they are liable to dream that their wishes have come true – quite falsely, as it transpires. This is because their conscious desires, their ego, has forced an entry into the closed territory of the *Personal unconscious mind* and taken over the dreaming process, hoping to influence events. The normal dreaming process by way of the *Inner feelings* will have been usurped, or short-circuited, or pre-empted, resulting only in false hope.

WITCH   *A woman with unpleasant characteristics*

Some women may think of 'witch' in terms of 'wicca', in the sense of 'personal goddess' or even 'female empowerment', but this is not the significance of the dream witch. The dream witch is the female counterpart of a demon or a devil, and is a manifestation of the *Shadow*. This frightening character will consist of matters that have been pushed into the *Personal unconscious mind*, thoughts, feelings and impressions that seemed unacceptable to the conscious awareness: all the disturbing ideas and negative emotions that should have been dealt with as they arose, but were denied recognition. These matters will have been gathering strength until they emerge in dreams in this guise; they may be identified as a 'night hag', or nightmare.

See also: DEMON; GODDESS; NIGHTMARE

WOLF

Over the centuries wolves have been demonised and given a bad name, as all wild dogs tend to be, although they are probably not an actual risk to humans. A 'wolf' can mean a womanising man; a 'wolf in sheep's clothing' is a hidden danger; to 'keep the wolf from the door' is to avoid starvation; to 'throw somebody to the wolves' is to make a scapegoat of them, and a 'wolf pack' can refer to any marauding gang. All these meanings may be associated with the wolf as a dream symbol: it implies something fearful that we cannot control.

See also: ANIMALS; DOG

World dream

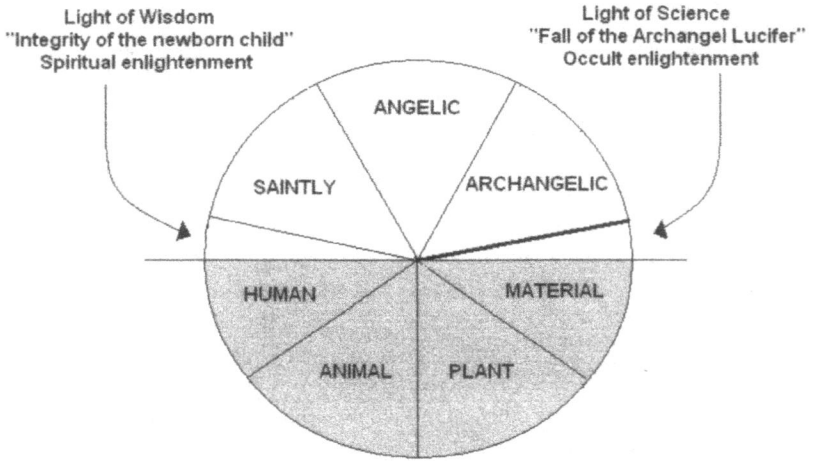

This world-scale mandala is a diagram of the *Cycle of creation*, and it is significant when considering the *Cycle of the dreaming self*, because it is the basic background to all our dreams, as well as the whole life of nature. Look at it in relation to the world in space. Above the horizon all is bathed in light; below all is in darkness. Sunrise, or the east, is to the left. Sunset, or the west, is on the right. The cycle of creation runs in a clockwise direction, set into motion, we could say, by the archangelic section (the 'fall of Lucifer'), and beginning with bare earth and solid rock. This basic state begins to support plant life; then animal life; and finally human life, and the cycle should continue. A newborn child emerging from the light enters the human zone (as the human race leaving the 'Garden of Eden') and aiming towards the benefits of civilisation available in the material zone, is drawn down towards that goal. Although necessary for civilisation, materiality is not the ideal spiritual condition for people, and having reached their material goal and acquired all the benefits they need, their best plan is to link up, on the inner dimension, with the cycle of creation and start back through the world of nature to attain the truly human level again. Having finally reached the point of birth and regaining the light, they will have been 'born again' in the Christian sense, and their progress will from then on be heavenwards. One way to begin the return journey on the inner plane is to start recording and listening to our dreams. This is the true function of dreams, because the *Dawn dream* of the world is the perfection of the human psyche.

Worried dreams

A dream may of course reflect a worry that is already present in the waking mind, but this will then have the nature of a *Wish-fulfilment dream* in its negative form stemming from the dreamer's ego, worried about some specific problem, and probably accompanied by disturbed sleep. The dreams themselves, though 'worried', will probably be fragmentary and nonsensical.

Worry   (A theme mood)

Quite distinct from the 'worried dream' (see above), worry as a theme mood, particularly upon waking, is normally associated with an imbalance of inner contents, the negative outweighing the positive. The dream will probably display elements of the *Shadow*, and will need interpreting very thoughtfully. Worry invariably ensues when a person, for whatever reason, finds himself or herself unable to follow his or her own inner contents, their true character, whether this is 'good' or 'bad'.

X

XENOPHOBIA

The fear or unreasonable hatred of foreigners as a dream theme has unfortunately become more common since the terrorist atrocities of recent times. As a dream symbol it involves becoming alarmed by some unknown and seemingly suspicious figure or figures approaching or surrounding the dreamer. Sometimes it is little more than apprehension: a feeling of being threatened by someone who may or may not actually appear in the dream. This falls into the category of dream *Opponent*, or more specifically a dream *Assailant* – an actual threat from a real person or thing. There is also an element of the dream *Adversary*, because the root of this fear may lie within the dreamer's own psyche, without involving an actual threat. If there is a lesson to be learnt from a xenophobic dream, it must be to avoid unreasonable attitudes and behaviour, or un-thought-out reactions aimed at perceived outsiders.

See also: BURGLAR; ENEMY; Fearfulness; GHOST

Y

Yin and yang

In Chinese philosophy the bright awareness of the masculine yang overrides the dark receptiveness of the feminine yin. This forms a useful symbol of our conscious awareness during the waking day, contrasted with the unconscious mind operating during the sleeping night. Matters which cannot be dealt with by the conscious mind tend to be pushed into the receptive area of the yin where they are stored, collated, reassembled, and finally re-presented in a new and more acceptable form by way of dreams.

YOKE   *A work-device for the shoulders*

This is an ancient symbol of servitude, slavery, drudgery, forced labour, and the general feeling of being exploited and hard done by. It often appears in marital dreams, particularly when the female of the relationship feels used and unappreciated. In dreams it may appear simply as a carved piece of wood unrecognised at first, or something to be carried on the shoulder. It may appear in the form of a wedding present of uncertain usage

See also: LOST; OBSTACLES; TOWER

Z

ZOO *A place where non-domestic animals are kept*

In a sense, people are animals, being largely governed by animal-type instincts and automatic reactions, and a dream zoo may represent the animal instincts of people in general. The symbol may appear in a dream when the dreamer has moved to a new area, a new job, a new school, a new type of society, where the other people involved seem to be less moral and more sexually expressive than had been expected. They are behaving 'like a lot of animals'. This depends on the dreamer's perceptions of others. But as a dream symbol the zoo could be reflecting the *World dream*. Even the 'plant' section of the world dream is a step above the normal soul-level of mankind, which is solidly material. The 'animal' section is quite well advanced, so as a dream symbol involving the dreamer, the zoo could represent a desirable place to be, and an ideal stepping-off point from which ambitions could well be achieved.

See also: ANIMALS; FARM

INDEX

abandonment 11
abbey 12
abuse 13
abyss 14, 15, 16
accident 16, 17
accusations 18
acne 18
acrobatics 19
acting, actors 19, 20, 21, 115, 116, 210
Adler, Alfred 21
adversary 22
advice 22
agility 24
altar 24, 25
analysing dreams 25, 26, 32, 33, 101-107, 163-170, 193
ancient relics 30
angel 26, 27
  avenging 27
anger 27, 28, 41, 42, 141
animals 28, 29, 59, 82, 97, 114, 123, 145, 183, 192, 202, 223, 228
antiques 31, 174
archaeology 31
archetype 22, 32, 33, 34, 36, 71, 142, 143, 185, 186, 222
argument 189
art 33, 34, 179
assailant 34
autumn 35

baby 36, 71, 72
baggage 161, 162
ball 37, 38
ballet 38
balloon 39
bamboo 40
barn 40, 41, 146, 205

barrier 126, 142, 177, 218
basement 69, 70
battle 41, 42
battlements 42
bees 144
betrayal 11
Biblical dreams 42-51
  barley cake 42, 43
  cows by the Nile 45, 46, 105
  Mary's pregnancy 42
  Nebuchadnezzar's idol 46-49
    tree 49-51, 106, 107
  Pharaoh's baker 44, 45, 56
    butler 44
  Solomon's visitation 43
  sun, moon and stars 43
  three wise men 42
  wheat sheaves 43, 44
birds 51-52, 77, 110, 180
blame 13, 18
blood 52, 53
boat 53, 54
bog 54, 55
bones 55, 202
books 55, 56, 159, 160
bread 56, 57
bridge 57, 58
broom 58
bugs 59, 149
bull 59
bullying 60
bulrushes 60-61
burglar 61, 62
burial 62

cactus 63
calendar 63
candle 64
car 17, 18, 64, 65, 66, 108
carnival 66, 67

229

carving 67
castle 42, 130
cathedral 68
cave 68, 69
cellar 69, 70
chasing 70, 71
child, children 36, 71, 72
church 12, 73
climbing 73, 74, 157, 172, 173
clock 75
clothes 76, 123, 141, 175, 215
clouds 77
cockerel 77
coldness 133, 137, 203
collective intelligence 78
collective unconscious mind 79
conscience 80
corpse 31, 62, 81, 90, 202
cow 45, 82, 105
crocodile 82
crossroads 83
crystals 83
cup 84

dam 87
dance, dancing 38, 87, 88
darkness 88, 112, 214
darts 88, 89
death 31, 62, 81, 90, 134, 139
demon 16, 90
desert 91, 198
diary 63
dice 92
digging 31, 62, 92, 93
dirt 93, 111, 109, 173
diving 96
doctor 96, 97
dog 97
doll 97, 98
dolphins 98
door 98, 99
dragon 100

dream re-entry 193, 194
dress 76, 215
drinking 84
driving 17, 108
drowning 108
dungeon 109
dust 109

eagle 110
earth mother 110
earthquake 111
eating 111, 123, 128, 129
echo 112
eclipse 112, 113
eggs 113
elephant 114
embroidery 114, 115
embryo 115
emotion in dreams 16, 23, 27, 33,
    53, 79, 87, 91, 95, 108,
    120, 124, 141, 144, 147,
    148, 152, 153, 161, 175,
    198, 199, 211, 219, 225
enemy 22, 34, 117, 177, 178
entry 98, 99, 136
escaping 117, 118
exam 119
excrement 120

facade 121
factory 121, 122
falling 15, 122
  leaves 35
farm 123
fashions 123, 124
fear 124, 132, 133, 144, 209, 210
feast 125
feet 125
fence 126
filth 93, 94, 120
fish, fishing 126

230

flexibility 19, 24, 38
floating 39, 127, 137
flowers 127, 160
flying 127, 128, 137
fog 123, 170
food 128, 129
ford 129
forest 129
fortress 42, 130
fossils 130
fountain 131
Freud, Sigmund 116, 131, 132
frost 133
fruit 133
fugitive 70, 71, 117, 118, 134
funeral 62, 134, 139, 160

gale 146
games 37, 38, 92, 184, 185
gardening 221
gateway 136
ghost 136
ghostly building 12
gift 136, 137
glacier 137
glider 137
goddess 138
gold 138
gorge 138, 139
grave 139, 140

hat 141
heart 52, 53
hedge 142
helplessness 21, 142
hero 142, 143
hole 14, 183
holly 143, 144
holy place 24, 74
honey 144
horse 145
hospital 145

hotel 145, 146
hurricane 146
hut 146

idol 147
illness 52, 53, 96, 146
incense 147, 148
indecision 157, 160
inferiority complex 21
insects 59, 149
insults 13
intuition 127, 150, 176

jetty 151
jewels 152
journey 152, 191
judge, judgment 119, 153
junction 153, 154
Jung, Carl Gustav 32, 154, 155
junk 198, 199

king 156
kite 156

labyrinth 157
ladder 157
lake 158
lameness 158
laughter 25, 159
laundry 159
lavatory 212
library 55, 56, 159, 160
lilies 160
limping 125, 158
lost 11, 15, 91, 95, 99, 160, 170
lucid dreaming 80, 161
luggage 161, 162

machinery 163
mandala 163-169
market place 169
marriage 130, 212, 227

231

marsh 54, 55
memorial 171
mist 170
monster 16, 82, 100, 171
monument 171, 204, 207
moon 171, 172
mountain 74, 172, 173
mud 54, 55, 173
museum 174
myth-making dreams 71, 174

naked 175
needlework 114, 115
night 88
nightmare 175
nonsense dreams 99, 118, 120

obstacles 177
opponent 177, 178

painting 33, 34, 179
parade 66, 67, 187
paralysis, sleep 180
parasites 59
parrot 180
path 181
pearl 181
perfume 147, 148
personal unconscious mind 14, 15, 16, 182
pets 29, 97
phantom 136
pier 151
pig 183
pimples 18
pit 14-16, 183
plant nature dreams 21, 184
playing 37, 38, 40, 92, 184, 185
ploughing 185
police 185, 186
pond 158
porpoise 98

precious object 24, 25, 30
precipice 186
present 136, 137
procession 66, 67, 187
pursuit 70, 71, 117, 118, 134

quarrel 189
queen 189, 190
questionnaire 190

rail journey 191
rainbow 191, 192
rats 192
reading 55, 56, 159, 160
recurring dreams 193
reeds 60, 61
reincarnation dreams 150, 194, 195
REM 192
river 129, 196
road 196
robber 61
rocks 197
role playing 19, 20, 21
rooster 77
royalty 156, 189, 190, 211
rubbish 15, 198, 199
ruined building 12, 13, 73, 197
running 70, 71, 117, 118, 134

sacred 24, 25
sadness 198
sailing 53, 54
sand 198
sandwiches 56, 57
scrapheap 198, 199
sea 199, 219
self 85, 86, 113, 116, 117, 121, 127, 163-170, 181, 182, 200, 203
sexual dreams 201, 220
shack 146

shadow 34, 82, 88, 90, 97, 109, 132, 133, 154, 175, 201
shed 40, 41, 146
ship 53, 54
skeleton 31, 55, 202
sky 77
sleep paralysis 180
snake 202, 203
snow and ice 203
somersaults 19, 24
statue 67, 204
stitching 114, 115
stepping stones 204
stones 197, 205
stone circle 205
store 40, 41, 205
storm 54, 146
sun 112, 206
sundial 207
sweeping 58
swimming 96

teeth 209
theatre 210
thief 61, 62
thorns 63, 143, 144, 210
throne 211
tidal wave 211, 212
toilet 212
tower 212, 213
travelling 152, 191, 196
treasure 138, 152, 181, 213
trees 129
tsunami 211, 212
tunnel 214

uncertainty 83, 99, 153, 154
uncharacteristic behaviour 79
unconscious mind 14, 15, 16, 78, 89, 93, 109, 151, 185, 186
unemployment 215
uniform 215

valley 216
vase 216
vehicle 17, 64, 65, 66, 108
viaduct 57, 58
volcano 217

walking 125, 181
wall 218
war 41, 42
warning dreams 219
water 219, 220, 221
weeding 221
windy 146
wise person 222
witch 223
wolf 223
work 121, 122
world dream 26, 28, 84, 85, 110, 165, 166, 224, 225
worry 31, 79, 225

xenophobia 226

yoke 227

zoo 228

THE KEY TO DREAM ANALYSIS

About the Author

Ray Douglas has been studying and interpreting dreams for the past fifty years, and he advises everyone who can do so to take an active interest in their own dream life. They will discover that their dreams become more and more meaningful as they begin to understand them better. People who are spiritually orientated will find the most amazing insights through their studies, and in equal measure their lives will be directed heavenwards. Those who are not so inclined will discover the truth of Sigmund Freud's assertion, that "the interpretation of dreams is the royal road to knowledge of the unconscious activities of the mind", and discover, as Freud's associate Carl Gustav Jung discovered, that this road leads to what he called psychological individuation – the process of becoming a uniquely whole, integrated person.

Ray Douglas was the first to formulate what he sees as the progressive development of dreams throughout the period of sleep, from the fragmented, chaotic dozing dreams of evening, to the completed, highly significant dreams that arrive just before dawn. He was also the first to relate the substance of our dreams with the world of nature and the natural cycle of creation, 'the great world dream' or the secret life of Gaia – our world seen as a vast, living, self-regulating organism. Once we begin to take an interest in our own dreams they become lifted above the mundane and open the way to rarefied knowledge. There is more to the process of dreaming than meets the eye, and it pays to take our dream lives seriously!

Other dream books by Ray Douglas include: *Dreams and the Inner Self;* and *Decoding Your Dreams.*

www.ingramcontent.com/pod-product-compliance
Lightning Source LLC
Chambersburg PA
CBHW060507090426
42735CB00011B/2139